Praise for **No Fear–No Death**

"With *No Fear–No Death*, Dr. Barry Kerzin makes us a wonderful gift: the insightful and moving testimony of his exploration of the path of fearless compassion, inner freedom and selfless wisdom. Anyone wondering "What am I here for?" will be delighted by reading this wonderful book."

–Matthieu Ricard, author of *Altruism, The Power of Compassion to Change Yourself and the World*

"Dr. Barry's story is gripping, and the teachings he humbly and humorously transmits are life-saving! It is a great introduction to the wisdom of freedom and compassion for others—the two wings of the great bird of true happiness! I'm sure you will enjoy this book as much as I do!"

–Robert Thurman, Professor of Indo-Tibetan Buddhalogy; author of *Man of Peace: The Illustrated Life Story of the Dalai Lama of Tibet*

"This extraordinary book is the product of Barry Kerzin's entire life, as a human being who knew suffering and loss early in life, as a medical doctor, and as a Buddhist monk. It is rare to live one's way into such a confluence of rigorous trainings in different ways of knowing and being, and be able to bring to life for others the essence of what one has tasted and learned directly oneself in such a remarkable synthesis. This book stands as a testimony to deeply human ways of investigating the realms of what we know and what we don't know and don't know that we don't know, for the benefit of all."

–Jon Kabat-Zinn, author of *Full Catastrophe Living* and *Coming to Our Senses*

"This extraordinary memoir and guide captures the journey and insights of a western trained physician and an ordained Buddhist monk. Barry is a great soul and his warmth and love come through in this volume."

–Abraham Verghese, author of *Cutting for Stone*

"I've known Barry Kerzin for many decades now. What a pleasure to read his new book on the Buddhist path to happiness. He offers us his personal story with its' serious challenges, and in plain English he shares with us what he has learned through his experiences as a beginning meditator to his present life as a monk and physician to His Holiness the Dalai Lama. These are profound and accessible teachings that will be of great help and encouragement to the beginner and longtime practitioner."

—Richard Gere, actor and activist

"A practical guide to Tibetan Buddhist meditation practice and philosophy that will be of interest to all those who wish to learn more about this great wisdom tradition, written by an American physician who became a monk. Sprinkled with personal stories and reflection, this book provides a toolkit for living a fulfilling life!"

—Richard J. Davidson, co-author of *Emotional Life of Your Brain* and *Altered Traits* and founder of the Center for Healthy Minds, University of Wisconsin-Madison

"In an age when white nationalism seeks a stronghold in the United States and populism challenges globalization internationally; in a time when the 'me generation' has been institutionalized and codified by narcissistic leaders of our age; the Venerable Barry Kerzin—physician, spiritual teacher, and friend to humanity—invites us to walk a different path: emptiness through meditation is the antidote to our frenzied egoism, and understanding ourselves as a global interconnected family leads us to find the 'meaning of life' through 'great' compassion for one another. As meditation *plays* with medicine, and wisdom *dances* with whimsy, Dr. Kerzin uncovers the key to a happy life."

—"The Rev" (Bryan Fulwider) from *Friends Talking Faith* with *The Three Wise Guys*, WMFE 90.7 FM, Orlando, Florida

NO FEAR
NO DEATH

NO FEAR
NO DEATH

The transformative power of compassion

BARRY KERZIN, M.D.

With a Foreword by
His Holiness the Dalai Lama

White Cloud Press
Ashland, Oregon

White Cloud Press books may be purchased for educational, business, or sales promotional use. For information, please write:

Special Market Department
White Cloud Press
PO Box 3400
Ashland, OR 97520
Website: www.whitecloudpress.com

Interior design by Christy Collins, Constellation Book Services

First edition: 2018

Printed in the United States of America

18 17 18 19 20 21   10 9 8 7 6 5 4 3 2 1

Library of Congress Cataloging-in-Publication Data

Names: Kerzin, Barry, author.
Title: No fear, no death : the transformative power of compassion / by Barry Kerzin, MD ; with a foreword by His Holiness the Dalai Lama.
Description: Ashland : White Cloud Press, 2018.
Identifiers: LCCN 2017053906 | ISBN 9781940468655 (pbk.)
Subjects: LCSH: Religious life--Buddhism. | Spiritual life--Buddhism. | Compassion--Religious aspects--Buddhism. | Buddhism--Doctrines.
Classification: LCC BQ7775 .K485 2016 | DDC 294.3/5699--dc23
LC record available at https://lccn.loc.gov/2017053906

MIX
Paper from
responsible sources
FSC® C011935

Contents

Foreword

The Venerable Dr. Barry Kerzin has been a friend of mine for almost thirty years. His skills as a physician mean not only that he has been helpful to me, but that he has also been of comfort to the many patients who have come into his care. The kindness of the doctors treating him when he fell ill as a boy sparked his ambition to become a doctor himself. Later, losing his mother and then his wife after a long struggle with cancer led to a period of recklessness that culminated in a serious exploration of what it is to be a human being and how we are to make our lives meaningful.

The Buddha's rational approach to reality, examining the causes of problems and seeking a remedy for them, appeals to people with a scientific turn of mind. Dr. Barry found himself drawn to the teachings of the Buddha and was eventually inspired to be ordained as a monk.

Naturally, there are teachings of the Buddha to be found in the scriptures, but there are also those that are rooted in the living experience of those who take them to heart. In this book, Dr. Barry shares with readers not only what he has learned and understood from reading and listening to teachers, but also how he has changed in trying to put his learning into practice. I admire the honesty and transparency this entails, which I am sure readers will value too.

His Holiness the Dalai Lama
Dharamsala, India
August 1, 2017

Chapter 1

Beginnings

Swept by the current of the four powerful rivers
(birth, aging, sickness, and death),
tied by the strong bonds of karma so hard to undo,
caught in the iron net of self-grasping,
completely enshrouded in the darkness of ignorance,
born and reborn in boundless cyclic existence,
ceaselessly tormented by the three miseries,
thinking of your mothers in this condition,
generate the supreme mind of enlightenment.

–Je Tsongkhapa, *The Three Principles of the Path*

I was born in Hollywood—my mother and father were on the way to a Halloween party and she said to him, "You know what. I don't think I should go to this party; you better take me to a hospital, I am going into labor." And the next day, on November 1, 1947, I was born. The name of the hospital was Good Samaritan Hospital. Maybe somebody knew I was going to be a bad boy and they'd better get me born in Good Samaritan—on the right side of the tracks. And I was born on All Saints' Day. I don't know why those things happened; I don't think they have anything to do with anything, but there you have it!

When I was young I was plagued—really plagued—by two questions. And I think many other people have had similar experiences; I suspect that if you are reading this book you have been similarly plagued, perhaps now, or possibly when you were young, maybe both. One question just kept coming up. It wasn't something I did intentionally, all this introspection. I was not some young Socrates questioning everything, but I was obsessed with answering the question, Who am I? Really, who am I? And of course I didn't have any answers, but the question just kept coming up again and again. I think I was six years old or so when that started. And this line of inquiry led to the second big question that kept coming up for me: What am I doing here? What's my life really all about?

By the time I got to high school, the questions remained, so I joined a philosophy club, thinking I might find the answers to my questions through philosophical inquiry. Our school was lucky to have a wonderful teacher from South America who had taught philosophy at a university in Chile but wasn't able to get his credential for teaching at the university level here in the States. So we were lucky to have him at our high school teaching Spanish, but really his interest was philosophy. He formed a philosophy club and I was eager to see what answers I might find via philosophy. My questions were addressed to some degree, but not to any great satisfaction. It was about this time that a number of books on Zen Buddhism came to me, and they moved me deeply. One was *The Way of Zen* by Alan Watts, and another was *An Introduction to Zen Buddhism* by

D. T. Suzuki. I was drifting, but there was clearly something like a path forming before me, though it would take more years and more searching before it became evident. Elements of clarity would take hold slowly.

In my younger years three important events shaped my future. First, when I was eleven years old I had an abscess in my brain. It caused me to fall into a coma, and I nearly died. The abscess ate away part of my brain and overlying bone in my skull. This is my internal rationalization for having difficulty learning new languages, for Broca's area in my brain was involved—that is a major area for speech development. Two years later, when I was thirteen years old, they decided to put a plastic plate in my left upper forehead to protect my brain. The neurosurgeon who operated on my brain four times literally saved my life. His care and compassion had a profound impact on me. I had great love for him. He was my hero, and I wanted to be like him. So from that age I felt the first stirring of a calling: I wanted to be a doctor. It was not an intellectual thing—it was deep in my heart and came to influence my choices as a teenager and a young adult.

Second, when I was in my mid-twenties my mother died of ovarian cancer. Not only did I lose a loving mother, but I also lost a refuge. She was my protector. I had felt secure knowing that if I were ever in deep trouble, she would always be there for me. When I developed the brain abscess mentioned above, I was very sick, and my mother was there with me, at my side throughout it all. I don't think I could have pulled through without her presence and love. Losing her, I also lost my security net. From then on I had to fend for myself.

And third, when I was in my early thirties, my wife Judy also died of ovarian cancer. During the nearly four years of her battle with cancer we became so close emotionally that her pain was my pain and mine, hers. We merged. Then she died and my life spiraled down. For several years I became reckless, nearly losing my life in a trekking accident, in a kayak accident, and in a scuba diving accident. I was pushing the limits, flirting with death, compelled to this recklessness by the wounding of the loss of the two women I had been closest to.

Moving through this time of recklessness, gradually I found myself in a search for a deeper meaning to my life. I returned to my early years of asking the big questions, Who am I, and why am I here? These continued into adolescence and early adulthood. But it was with the loss of my wife Judy that an intense search began to provide answers to these questions.

It became a preoccupation with me to find meaning during these turbulent times, in the late 1960s and early '70s. At the University of California, Berkeley, I started out as a premed student. I studied chemistry, math, biology, and related subjects for two years. I didn't like it, so I switched to philosophy, hoping to find some answers that made sense to me. Alas, the philosophy department did not address my questions in a way that made sense or satisfied my inner turmoil, even though I left Berkeley with my BA in philosophy in 1976. I then returned to the passion of my teen years: becoming a doctor. I enrolled to study medicine at the University of Southern California. Judy and I married three days before I started medical school. Then just after I completed my family medicine residency at Ventura County Medical Center, Judy was diagnosed with advanced ovarian cancer.

Our world looked bleak, but we never gave in. Realistic optimism and love gave us strength. There was no time for superficialities. Judy and I spent some of the most meaningful moments together during that time. Finishing a long day of medical practice in Ojai, California, I would drive ninety minutes to be with her at UCLA hospital, only to return home, go to bed, and repeat the process the next day. She spent maybe one quarter of her three and a half years of battling ovarian cancer in the hospital. When I lost her, I realized I must do something more with my life.

So in the wake of Judy's death my search intensified. I now had a chance to fulfill my desire to go to India. Judy had not been too keen on going there, but now with her passing and my intensified search for meaning, I headed east. In 1984, I made my first trip to India, Sri Lanka, and Nepal, a trip that lasted eight months. This happened about six months after Judy passed. I was looking for something more—I didn't know what. I traveled around the region, met some wonderful lamas, and heard some wonderful teachings, and the hook was in. I didn't realize it then, but the hook was in. And I liked it. While in Asia, I spent several months in Kopan Monastery. When I heard Lama Zopa teach on "emptiness," I was profoundly touched. At lunch, sitting on top of a building, dangling my feet, I started to hallucinate—without drugs. Among other things I saw a huge Native American tepee. I saw myself crawling up the side to the top, to look inside. I knew the reason, the meaning of this experience. It was to see what was inside myself. When I got to the top and looked inside, there was nothing. Actually nothing! I freaked out. My body trembled, my pulse raced, and I started sweating. Intense fear enveloped me. I deeply felt I was nonexistent. Others came to help, and I was slowly taken down a simple ladder made of a log with notches and laid on the ground. I slowly came out of it. The experience recurred, but less intensely, for some months.

Later, I had the precious opportunity to ask His Holiness the Dalai Lama whether I was going crazy or what? He reassured me and said it was an authentic experience but that I went a little far by negating everything. Emptiness experience, he said, is close to that, but with some conventional reality remaining. This is apparent, he said, when we arise from the emptiness meditation. I was relieved and felt a special closeness to him.

After that, I took a job as an assistant professor in Seattle at the University of Washington School of Medicine. This ended up being a four-year stint. Slowly, the recklessness subsided. I met Gen Lamrimpa, a Tibetan spiritual leader and hermit who lived in seclusion not far from Dharamsala, India, the spiritual center of Tibetan Buddhism in exile. Genla lived in the mountains above Dharamsala in lifetime retreat. Due to his incredible love and kindness, he came to Washington State to lead meditation retreats and teach. I became his driver and student, and when his two years' stay in Washington was over I accompanied him back to Dharamsala, where I stayed initially for six months, then kept extending my stay now for twenty-nine years.

Several years later, my friend Alan Wallace returned from the first Mind and Life conference in Dharamsala with a message from the His Holiness the Dalai Lama. This was October 1987. His Holiness was requesting a Western-trained physician to come to Dharamsala to coordinate various medical systems for the purpose of making them available for any sick person, but not to combine them into a single system. This resounded loudly in my heart and mind. Having saved up two months of vacation leave from the University of Washington, I was off to Dharamsala. It was a match made in heaven. The following year I moved there, thinking I would be there six months or so then back to Seattle. Twenty-eight years later I am still there. The traditional Tibetan medicine doctors wanted to rigorously research their medical system. We chose a research project to examine the benefit of Tibetan medicine on improving high blood pressure. In this hands-on way I taught them rudimentary research methodology.

Now back in India, for a number of years beginning in 1989, I saw Gen Lamrimpa several times a week, getting advice on meditation and on life. He was an extraordinary meditator: he spent his life in meditation. I was had been so fortunate to serve as his driver in Seattle. He was extremely precious, extremely kind—someone I have a tremendous feeling of indebtedness to. He passed away near Gangtok, Sikkim, in 2003. I spent many months with him at that time helping with his cancer treatment.

Several of his teachings have been made into books. *Calming the Mind; How to Practice Shamatha Meditation; Transcending Time*, and others.[1] He was a Kalachakra master who lived as a hermit in a simple one-room hut above Dharamsala, in the mountains above His Holiness the Dalai Lama's residence. Every year, the monks of Namgyal Monastery cycle through different tantric practices for the year. In the third month by the lunar calendar at the time of the full moon, they practice the Kalachakra *sadhana* (instructions for practice—a practice manual). For several days they practice the long sadhana, which lasts up to fourteen hours. Only a few of the top masters of the Kalachakra tantra system are invited to participate with the monks of Namgyal Monastery. Gen Lamrimpa was one of the great meditation masters who were regularly invited, along with Kirti Tsenshab Rinpoche.

I was so fortunate to get to drive this outstanding meditation master around Seattle years before. I got to know him and he had a profound effect on me. Mostly in very positive ways, but also in some not so good ways. For a number of years, I thought I was a yogi. He was a yogi. He ate but he didn't have to eat; he would breathe but he almost didn't have to breathe. He had a lot of control over the internal elements. He was a highly evolved meditation master. And somehow I thought that since I was his student I should follow his practice, and I didn't take care of my body. I didn't eat very well and I didn't sleep that much. I did this for years and as a result my health declined. Three major bones broke within one year and I was diagnosed with severe osteoporosis. I am doing a lot better now. I am eating much better, but it was a mistake to think I was a yogi like my teacher.

So, as I have mentioned, when Genla finished teaching for two years in Washington State, he went back to his hermitage in the mountains above Dharamsala and I accompanied him. At immigration in the airport in Delhi, he was stopped due to insufficient documents. Being rather bold in those days, my rebellious Berkeley background still a part of my social repertoire, I went back out through immigration to stay with him. The next morning, I reached the Dalai Llama's representative by phone—an old landline from the 1950s—and a car plus driver showed up shortly. We were given twenty-four hours to get the appropriate stamps. Riding around in an old Ambassador car, we scurried around Delhi from one bureaucratic office to another. Finally, at five p.m. we had all the documents signed . . . except one. Genla said to go to the last office even though we all knew it had closed and hour before. But Genla had clairvoyance. When we arrived at the last office, the door was open, so we entered. In the very back of the building was one woman. I explained our predicament and, almost miraculously, she signed the last document, allowing Genla to return as a refugee to his home in India, away from his true home—Tibet.

My time with Genla was precious time in the presence of a true master of meditation. It had the most profound effect, turning my life toward meditation, Buddhist study, and, eventually, monastic life—all of which filled me with much joy.

Chapter 2

Awakening

Irrigators regulate the rivers;
fletchers straighten the arrow shaft;
carpenters shape the wood;
the wise control themselves.
−The Buddha, *The Dhammapada*

I am often asked how to attain happiness, and this is an important question for all of us. First, we must differentiate in our own lives pleasure from happiness. Pleasure is sensory experience. So it does not last, and can even turn into its opposite: pain. Happiness is inner peace and calmness of mind and heart. From a Buddhist perspective, we cannot separate the idea of happiness from Buddhist wisdom. In this regard, Buddhism is often likened to a great soaring bird. And the bird has two wings to keep it afloat: wisdom and compassion. And it turns out that these are not as separate as the "two wings of a bird" analogy might suggest. In fact, they are two sides

9

of the same coin, wisdom and compassion, both of which are necessary for attaining happiness. I will have more to say about compassion later. For the moment let us begin with wisdom.

The Buddha offered a number of metaphors for reality. He said life is like a dream; he said life is like a mirage. Life is like a reflection, we could say, of our face in the mirror. He talked about a reflection of the moon in a still body of water, a lake. And he provided other metaphors.

Let's look at the dream metaphor. What did the Buddha mean when he said, "Life is like a dream"? When we dream, we engage with images. We may in fact have an image of a dear friend, a loved one. And in the dream we feel intense love for that friend. When we wake up we begin to rub our eyes and there's a mismatch. Are we in the dream? Are we waking up? Where's our friend? I still feel that warmth and love, but where's my friend? And as we wake up more and more we recognize there never was a friend; it was only an image in our dream. And so when we wake up from sleep and dream, it is as if that image of the friend and the feeling of love, which were so strong and so clear, just went poof. We recognize that it wasn't real. The friend was not really there. It was only an image in a dream. So our normal, deluded life is like believing the dream image to be true and real. When we awaken through understanding wisdom, we see "through" this. We recognize appearance to be like illusion. We break through the bubble of concepts and see reality as it is.

This does not mean nothing exists. Rather the distorted perceptions and conceptions are not reality. In this vein, the Buddha taught the two truths. In fact, the Buddha, Nagarjuna (d. 250 CE), and Nagarjuna's major disciples taught these two truths at the beginning of a discourse on wisdom. There is conventional truth and ultimate truth. Ultimate truth is emptiness. When we meditate on emptiness, nothing appears before the mind. Yet we are not "spaced out." Arising from that repeated meditation, appearances are there. But the difference is that now we do not take them to be real. We have deep conviction that they are like illusions. Conventional truth is what we normally take to be reality. As we deepen our understanding of the ultimate truth of emptiness, at the same time our understanding of conventional truth deepens. We begin to realize that these appearances of conventional reality are veiled reality. They are like illusions. Let's take an example. In ancient India there were "illusionists," or magicians. Using spiritual power and chanting mantras, they could create images of women, horses, and elephants, perhaps like a modern-day hologram. The audience believed these images to be real women, horses, and elephants. Ignorance hoodwinks us into believing images to be real. The magician, on the other hand, knows these images to be mistaken, without valid referent objects. A person walking by does not even see the images. This is like the Buddha, whose mind sees reality. The magician is like the person with some understanding of emptiness, but not to such a great extent. He knows these to be magical creations but he still reacts to them with emotion.

Buddha said that our understanding, our perception, our conception of reality is just like that. When we wake up and we begin to appreciate and experience the wisdom of emptiness, then we recognize that our current experiences of our self, others, and the world are all mistaken. They are not real. Just like an image in a dream as we wake up. They are merely creations of our mind, made up of words, language, and thoughts, just like the image in the dream.

Recognizing repeatedly the important similarity we share with others brings us closer to them. We feel a shared humanity, the profound sense that we are all brothers and sisters. At a deep level, we understand we are all the same. Regardless of whether we are male or female, young or old, from this country or culture or that country or culture, or have other differences, we all share this deep sameness of wanting to be well and not wanting to hurt. We relate as members of the large human family. No matter whether these people are friends, strangers, or even enemies, they will all feel close, like new friends or like brothers and sisters.

This illustrates the very important role played by the wisdom of emptiness. Examining the ego thoroughly becomes an important method of cultivating deeper, unbiased, universal compassion. This universal compassion is not based on others' response to us. It is not, "If they are kind, I will be kind; and if they are mean, I will be mean." Rather, it is based on a broader perspective than just our own ego, a thoughtful attitude cultivated from our inner mental consciousness. This broader perspective frees us from taking things personally. It gives us the freedom to act in an unbiased way. This is cultivated through wisdom. A broader attitude allows our compassion to spread out further, to more and more people and animals. Having this broader perspective, detached from our ego, does not mean being cold and aloof. Rather, it allows us to engage fully with others. Eventually, our compassion will spread to everyone equally. This is what is meant by "great compassion." "Great" refers to the number of those receiving our compassion, which eventually becomes almost limitless. At least, our attitude and feeling is closeness to all, supporting everyone like a brother or a sister.

The function of the unique Buddhist wisdom of emptiness is to lead us beyond taking our illusions as reality. Buddhist wisdom shows us the way to break our chronic habits and addictions of distorting and misperceiving reality. Due to strong self-grasping and strong self-cherishing, we cling to a distorted view of reality. So the ego becomes narcissistic. It feels as though it is the center of the world. Actually we are a "blip" within infinite universes embedded in infinite time! Self-grasping is an extreme exaggeration. It involves identifying and clinging to a distorted perception, thinking that what we perceive is real. This is especially true of egocentricity. We grasp our ego so tightly that we identify with this distorted perception of our ego as if it were our self. Wisdom breaks through the world of ignorance, which grasps at our self and things as real. Understanding, the fruit of wisdom, brings freedom. Uniting wisdom with compassion broadens and deepens our compassion, allowing it to cut suffering from its root. It deepens our ability to help others find deep, lasting inner happiness. Self-grasping and self-cherishing are self-centered and selfish, the opposite of wisdom and compassion. They are narcissistic, thinking we are the center of the world and that the whole world revolves around "me, me, me." We all fall into this narrow mindset nearly all the time. We get trapped in this ingrained habit. Certainly I do. It takes work to free our self from this strong preconception. Sometimes we are thinking about the welfare of others, but usually with selfish strings attached. Usually we are taking care of number one. We spend an inordinate amount of time thinking and planning for our own needs. We get trapped in this narrow-minded attitude of self-preoccupation.

The opposite of self-cherishing does not mean neglecting ourselves. Rather, it means adopting a wider perspective, recognizing the needs of others. When we focus on the hopes, needs, and welfare of others, an attitudinal paradigm shift takes place.

We begin deeply taking care of ourselves. By helping others and being concerned about others, we also reap the benefit. We feel more relaxed, open, and peaceful. A sense of meaning fills our life. We feel happy and more content.

Letting go of self-grasping is profound. Letting go of distorted perceptions brings a freedom that is delicious. All our perceptions, thoughts, and feelings are merely fabrications projected by our mind. Letting go of self-grasping brings us in line with how things actually are. This reality is much softer and gentler. It feels intricately interwoven. The world becomes systems of interrelationships. Everything feels balanced and joyous. It is the reality of interdependence. *Emptiness means interdependence.* Emptiness and interdependence reject the notion of a reality that is unchanging and independent. Both accept a reality that views everything as existing solely in relationship, only in interdependence with other things. Nothing is objectively real. Nothing exists from its own side. Everything is merely imputed, merely designated. This is Buddhist wisdom, beyond concepts.

Normally we see differences when we meet people, and we focus on these differences.

Those differences are very superficial. They are not very deep. Gender, race, age, how much hair, how little hair (none in my case)—so many differences we focus on—but what we miss is one important quality that we all share: We all want to be happy, don't we? We all want to feel well. And a corollary to that is that we don't want to hurt. None of us want to suffer. We all share that and yet we tend to forget that. We tend to look at those superficial differences. Of course there are differences, but this is more fundamental—this deep sense of wanting to be happy. It unites us deeply, as we are all members of the same human family.

So, based on this notion we can have an attitudinal shift from selfishness to concern for others. The more we remember that we all share the same desire for happiness, the closer we then feel to others. On the other hand, the superficial differences tend to separate us. They create artificial distance. So the more we remember this universal sameness, the more our attitude will shift from selfishness to concern for others—just through remembering, like a mantra, "We just all want to be happy. Just like me, she just wants to be happy. Just like me, he does not want to hurt."

We can then redefine who we are because our identity does not have to be limited to this body. This body does not even belong to us; it comes from the sperm and egg of our father and mother, yet we call it our own. Due to this profound interconnectedness and this new way of thinking, flexibility is fostered to redefine who we are, deeply. We are members of one human family. Just as we formerly artificially identified with the product of the sperm and egg of others, we have the freedom to shift our identity—to shift our identity to the whole human family.

We have the choice to think this way because this body has something to do with others and is not just mine, which we normally take to be the case. Therefore, we can shift this attitude of defining "I" and "me" as this body. We can shift it. It is our choice. We can shift this personal identity from me to We. Just as we formally identified our self with this body, we can expand the me to We, thus expanding our identity to the entire human family. Identifying our self with this body is too limiting. Even identifying with our family, or even this nation, is too limiting. His Holiness the Dalai Lama has been saying this again and again, that the notion of nationhood is old-fashioned. Nationhood was relevant in the twentieth century. But nationhood is no longer relevant in this twenty-first century. We are now so interconnected because of commerce and travel, because of education, because of communication, especially the Internet, that national boundaries are losing their significance and reason for being. And as we are all members of one human family, national boundaries become obsolete.

Here we are speaking of ignorance, of not knowing who we really are. Well, I say, I know who I am. I am Barry. But if we go a little deeper, who am I? We don't really know, and what we think is "I" is usually wrong. It is usually a distortion, either inflated or deflated. So, ignorance means not knowing reality correctly: not knowing who we are and not knowing the reality of the mind and not knowing the reality of the material world. We take appearances to be real. We assume appearances match something objective out there. This assumption solidifies our belief in an objective reality out there.

So we must "mind the gap." And what is the gap? We need to examine whether there is a gap between appearance and reality. Are appearances reflecting something real out there? Or are they just creations of the mind? Do appearances accurately map onto an objective reality, or not? We assume they do, although we rarely, if ever, think about this. Whatever appears to our mind we take to have a real referent object. Without thinking about it, we take it to be real. You get out of your car and step on the pavement. You don't think for a moment that the pavement is only a mental experience, a mental creation. We don't think there is no objectively real pavement. From the perspective of chemistry and physics, the pavement is made of atoms. The atoms are made up of 99.999999999999 percent empty space. The protons, neutrons, and electrons are infinitesimally small in comparison. The atom is made up of empty space. So when we get out of our car, we don't think that we are going to fall through empty space. Our experience, in this case of objective, solid ground, is mistaken; that is, the appearance is projected by our mind. It is not real; it is only a mental projection. This example from chemistry and physics is not the same as Buddhist wisdom, but it moves us closer to understanding emptiness by de-solidifying reality. More than that, it makes a crack in our understanding of a solid, monolithic, unchanging objective world. It dawns on us there may be a gap between what seems to appear and what is actually there, that is, reality.

Now, the pavement doesn't matter so much, but when we investigate our ego it is a big problem. For it is a mistake to not know who we are and to act on that mistake. We do that all the time. It brings great trouble. We get hurt and we hurt others, all because we don't know who we really are. Based on the assumption of an independent, objective ego, when someone says some bad words we get upset and maybe angry. When someone says something nice to us, we get inflated. This is the ignorance that I am talking about. It always leads to reacting with either attachment or aversion. Both throw us out of balance. Both rob us of our inner peace and joy.

The exact opposite of ignorance is wisdom. This is the wisdom of knowing who we really are. This is the wisdom of knowing reality correctly. In this way we begin to awaken. When wisdom overturns ignorance there are no more causes for attachment or aversion. Things are more peaceful, and there is more space and energy for concern for the welfare of others. There is more room for love and compassion. There is more room for deep relaxation, joy, and profound happiness.

Chapter 3

Self, Interdependence, and Wisdom

When "self" is conceived, "others" naturally arise;
the conception of self and others leads to
attachment and aversion; this in turn results in misery.

—Acharya Dharmakirti, seventh-century Buddhist master

A unitary, permanent, independent self is a mental fabrication; it is not real. This is the distorted ignorance of our self and the world. Due to this we artificially see the world as solid and separate—"I" and "it" and "us" and "them"—separating ourselves from others. We discriminate based on this artificial separation, mistakenly perceiving ourselves as separate and cut off. We conceive of all kinds of artificial boundaries and separations.

Buddhist wisdom shows us the way to break our habit of misperceiving reality, thinking everything is objective and independent. It moves us toward the understanding that everything is interdependent. Everything is complexly interwoven. This is true on the gross level, as in science, where everything is inter-related. On the subtle level, everything is inextricably related with its name. So something (only a name itself), which is similar to it the parts, acts as a base when a name is given. Out of this dependent relationship between the base (parts) and a designated name, something arises.

In the field of biology, food chains and symbiosis are based on interdependence. Climate change, affecting regions far apart, is another system based on interdependence. In the field of physics, subtleties of nature, the theories of quantum entanglement, and the general theory of relativity are based on interdependence. Einstein's general theory of relativity explains the relationship between gravity and space-time. Interdependence is also fundamental to the understanding of the origin of the universe.

All these various systems and fields require interdependence for their functioning. In fact functioning means interdependence—things in relationship, with the ability to change. Recognizing that relations of mutual dependence characterize so many aspects of our life moves us toward a more realistic understanding of the world we live in. It also helps us better negotiate our own place in this complex world. This kind of understanding is a strong catalyst for cultivating compassion, as it is more in tune with reality.

Recognizing interdependence reduces our selfishness, thereby enhancing our compassion. The ego is no longer seen as isolated. Rather it exists due to and within complex inter-dependent relationships. There is mother and father. There is family. There is society. On the subtle level, there is on one hand a body and a mind, and on the other hand someone called "Barry"—nothing more than a name. These two come together to create me! I am nothing more or less than that! Understanding interdependence gives us the panoramic view required to see the whole situation clearly. This allows us better decision making.

Usually, we are wrapped up in our own feelings. Feelings of hurt take center stage. We rarely move beyond our feelings and try to understand the feelings of the other person who has harmed us. What are the circumstances in their life that led them to become a bully? And what are the consequences for them of bullying others? If the other person were happy, there would be no reason for them to act in a hostile manner toward us. So what difficulties is that person facing?

When we think from this panoramic perspective, more understanding and compassion naturally arise. This wider perspective based on the understanding of interdependence is more balanced, offering a more complete picture. As self-centeredness decreases, more humility arises. And compassion is automatically enhanced, as on a balance scale. The ego and concern for others are inversely related, like a teeter-totter. When ego goes down, concern for others goes up. In this way, understanding interdependence increases our compassion.

Wisdom

This illustrates the very important role played by wisdom. Examining the ego thoroughly becomes an important method of cultivating deeper, unbiased, universal compassion. This universal compassion is not based on others' response to us. It is not that we are kind only when kindness is shown to us. Rather, it is based on a more detached, holistic, thoughtful attitude from our inner consciousness. Detachment frees us from taking things personally. It gives us the freedom to act in an unbiased way. This attitude is cultivated through wisdom. A detached attitude allows our compassion to spread out further, to more and more people. It does not mean neglecting others. In fact, it is just the opposite. It means reducing our egotistical attitude in favor of concern for others. There are many, many more others than single me. Eventually, our compassion will spread to everyone and all living beings equally. Again, this is what is meant by "great compassion." Our attitude encompasses all of these infinite living beings.

Everyone wants to be happy. No one wants pain. Recognizing repeatedly this similarity we share with others brings us closer to them. We feel a shared humanity. At a deep level, we understand we are all the same. Regardless of whether we are a man or a woman, young or old, or have other differences, we all share this deep sameness of wanting to be well and not wanting to hurt. We become a member of the large human family. No matter whether this person is a friend, stranger, or even an enemy, they will all feel like new friends. I am repeating this, as it is crucial to understand and implement in order to develop great compassion.

Adopting a wider perspective gives us the emotional space to distance our self from feelings of anger. Having emotional space, we learn not to identify with the anger. We can just let the feeling of anger go without clutching onto it as ours. We simply imagine the anger floating away like a cloud, drifting naturally across the sky. There is no need to identify with the anger as "me" or "mine." This is quite difficult to do when anger is full blown. So we train in recognizing the early signs of anger, such as frustration, irritability, fast heartbeat, fast breathing, and so on.

When people harm us in some way, it is helpful to recall that a vast array of factors have contributed to their behavior. This is the practice of skillful action: compassion in action guided by wisdom's adopting a broad perspective on the situation. When we face aggression or disrespect, it is worth considering why the aggressive or disrespectful people are acting that way. Very likely their behavior reflects difficulties they themselves are experiencing. This behavior could also reflect difficulties from their past. For example, they may be harboring dysfunctional family-of-origin issues. Often, dysfunctional strategies adopted during childhood, when we are trying to cope with unhealthy family dynamics, stay with us like a rotten apple at the bottom of the barrel. This rotten apple can spoil all the healthy apples nearby. These dysfunctional strategies often go unnoticed throughout our lives, although they often create turbulence beneath the surface. This turbulence can manifest as irritability, depression, sadness, anger, or other negative moods. These influence our relationships throughout life.

Similar emotional response patterns based on childhood dysfunctional strategies seem to surface again and again. Recognizing these patterns can modulate our instinct for revenge and blaming others. That other person is not actually my older brother, who bullied me when I was young, even though it feels similar. Furthermore, understanding similar negative family influences and difficulties in the person who harmed us makes it easier for us to understand that person, as well. Through understanding, we are more able to forbear and forgive. Given the right circumstances we might have caused the same harm to someone else.

The function of this unique Buddhist wisdom is to lead us beyond our illusions of a solid and fixed reality. Buddhist wisdom shows us the way to break our chronic habits of distorting and misperceiving reality. Due to strong self-grasping and strong self-cherishing, we cling to a distorted view of reality. So the ego needs the spotlight. It feels as though it is crying out to be the center of attention. We are nothing more than an itsy bitsy speck within infinite universes folded within beginningless time. When we look closer we cannot even find this "blip!" Self-grasping means identifying with and clinging to a distorted perception, thinking it is real. This is true of everything we perceive, but this self-grasping of our ego gets us into most of the trouble. We grasp it so tightly that we identify with this distorted perception of our ego as if it were our self.[1]

Wisdom breaks through our normal world, helping us to see it as like an illusion. Understanding brings freedom from suffering, for suffering is embedded in our distorted perceptions and conceptions. Uniting wisdom with compassion deepens our compassion, overturning the subtlest kind of suffering, which underpins all of our suffering. It deepens our ability to help others find genuine, lasting happiness. This key of wisdom unlocks the door to happiness. Self-cherishing is self-centered and selfish. It is narcissistic, thinking we are the center of the world and that the whole world revolves around "me, me, me." We all fall into this narrow mindset much of the time. We get trapped in this ingrained habit. Certainly I do. It takes work to free our self from this strong preconception. Sometimes we are thinking about the welfare of others. But usually we are taking care of number one. We spend an inordinate amount of time thinking about our own needs. We get trapped in this narrow-minded attitude, thinking mistakenly that it will bring happiness.

Trying to find more happiness actually leads to more dissatisfaction. The opposite of self-cherishing does not mean neglecting ourselves. Rather, it means adopting a wider perspective, recognizing the needs of others, thereby ensuring our own happiness. When we pay attention to the hopes and needs of others, something inside us shifts. Ironically, we start taking excellent care of ourselves. Even though it seems contradictory that by taking care of others we take maximal care of our self, helping and having concern for others actually benefits us greatly. We feel open and relaxed, filled with a sense of purpose to our life. We feel content and happy. The recipient of our compassion also feels good. This becomes one of those rare life situations in which both parties benefit—a so-called win-win situation.

Letting go of self-grasping is profound and brings a freedom one has never experienced before. This we have discussed in some detail above in chapter 2.[2] This reality born of wisdom is much softer and gentler. It feels intricately interwoven. The world becomes systems of relationships. Everything feels balanced and joyous. It is the reality of interdependence. Emptiness means interdependence. Both reject the notion of a reality that is unchanging and independent. Both accept a reality that views everything as existing solely in relationship, only in interdependence with other things; where there are no entities, rather processes, all born out of interdependence. On the deepest level this is dependent designation, or labeling. So from a name in conjunction with something like parts, although themselves not entities, arise all things including our self.

This understanding to some degree is shared by modern quantum physics. Both quantum physics and Buddhist science understand reality to be interdependent. There is nothing more than that. There are no solid entities. There are only relationships. Everything in the universe, the subatomic world, and our selves exists that way. Still, understanding interdependence theoretically is not the same as practicing and realizing it. Realization radically alters our life. We awaken to utter joy and a love and compassion that never quits.

The important expression of realizing interdependence is our behavior. We become patient, loving, and kind. A new sense of courage and strength overtakes us. Life becomes meaningful. Conversely, a strong sense of ego separates us from others. It creates an "us versus them" life struggle. The wisdom of interdependence reconnects us with others, like genuine brothers and sisters.

> *Life's struggles transform into joy and meaning –*
> *these are the teachings of the Buddha.*
> *Conflict and anger evaporate.*
> *Jealousy and competitiveness disappear.*
> *Our hearts open.*
> *Everyone we meet feels like a new friend.*
> *Mutual respect and trust blossom.*
> *Genuine friendship replaces artificiality.*
> *Everything hums with joy.*

Understanding and practicing wisdom is a lifelong endeavor. With it comes newfound love and compassion. Wisdom and compassion are two sides of the same coin. Both lead us, as well as others, to rich, meaningful lives. Both free us from the prisons of self-grasping and self-cherishing.

Chapter 4

Happiness

Why be unhappy about something
if it can be remedied?
And what is the use of being unhappy
if it cannot be remedied?
—Shantideva (Eighth century), *Bodhisattvachayavatara*

Let us return to the question of happiness, and here I need to
say that from a Buddhist perspective we have to recognize
that to a certain extent life is sad. In fact, all of unenlightened
existence is fraught with dissatisfaction, fraught with angst,
fraught with disappointment. Of course we have short periods
when the suffering is less intense. When we awaken we realize
how much we were suffering but are often unaware of the
depths. In a sense we have become habituated to angst. I don't
think there is a single person who has not experienced sadness
or suffering at some level. If we haven't we are not an ordinary
human. This is where the Buddha started his teachings, with
the fact that life is never fully satisfying.

As I noted in Chapter 1, there has been much suffering in my life, starting when I was a child of eleven stricken with a massive brain abscess. It was so serious that I fell into a coma and my parents began to grieve what they thought would be the loss of their first child. Then there was the loss of my mother and later my wife, during my early adult years.

With the passage of a little time, it is possible to change one's perspective on personal suffering and see the silver lining in the dark cloud. Experiencing our own suffering allows us to be in touch with others' suffering. Then compassion can arise. My serious illness led me to become a doctor, out of a motivation to help others the way my doctors helped me. Losing those close to me inspired a search for meaning in life and death. It led me on a spiritual journey and eventually to the monastic life. My good fortune and karma, coupled with his unlimited love and kindness, eventually led me to a close relationship with His Holiness the Dalai Lama.

The truth is, we do not need to be attached to our suffering. We can use our personal suffering to understand the suffering of others. This cultivates concern for others, which leads to love and compassion for others. We can release our self from sadness and suffering. In order to do this fully we need to employ the wisdom of emptiness. So in this way compassion and wisdom are closely intertwined. They are the two wings of the great soaring bird that is a metaphor for awakening—for enlightenment.

I have had the great fortune of spending a lot of time with His Holiness the Dalai Lama, and he is an amazing individual. I take care of him and as one of his doctors. Often I feel it is he who is taking care of me! As I do this service, I realize that this person has something very special and I want to know what it is. This man is truly happy even though he deals with so much suffering: People coming out of Tibet who have been tortured tell him horror stories and he listens compassionately and lovingly. People with sick and dying children consult him. People with devastating chronic physical and mental illness see him hoping for some miracle cure. And it doesn't faze him, in the sense that he doesn't get down. He responds with deep compassion infused with wisdom. So while there is genuine compassion, at the same time he doesn't take things too seriously. He recognizes people and things for what they are—like illusions—nothing to grasp onto and attach to. Similarly, his own self or ego—like an illusion—is not something to grasp at or get attached to.

So how do we learn to act more compassionately?

First, I have to say, as a doctor, that we have to take care of our bodies. We have to be physically healthy as best we can, but of course some things we can't control. In my case I let my physical health slide for many years, thinking I was a yogi, though I'm not. I didn't eat well and this behavior led to physical ailments. For over twenty years I was a strict vegetarian, though my childhood diet had included meat. Insidiously, I lost weight and strength. It happened so slowly, over years, that I did not recognize it until several minor falls led to my breaking three major bones. The doctors told me I had severe osteoporosis and advised better protein intake in addition to treatment specific to osteoporosis. After doing all the doctors recommended, I am much stronger and much healthier. Very occasionally I will supplement my vegetarian diet with some fish.

Here I want to mention some medical studies that show that happiness and caring have some relationship to good health. Several years ago an important research study looking at women with breast cancer concluded that positive mental states improve longevity. For the two groups of women with breast cancer, all the women in both groups received the standard recommended treatment. This included surgery, chemotherapy, radiation, hormonal modulation, and immunotherapy when indicated. One group of women with breast cancer additionally received TLC, tender loving care, and stress reduction. It turns out that the group that received the love was happier, with higher life satisfaction, which was expected. Not only were they happier, but unexpectedly they also lived longer. So it actually helped them in a variety of ways to live fuller lives, even when suffering from breast cancer.[1]

Many studies have now been done exploring the relationship between the immune system and compassion. The immune system is enhanced and gets stronger when we are happier. When we are not happy the immune system weakens. So what does the immune system do? First off it helps us fight infection and reduce inflammation. Compassion meditation has been shown to reduce stress and improve well-being. An important study showed enhanced immunological activity with reduced stress and increased compassion, demonstrated by lower serum cortisol levels and lower IL-6 (Interleukin-6) levels. Interleukin-6 is a complex system. Basically these levels are inversely proportional to a healthy immune system and to compassion. So lower levels of interleukin-6 mean a healthier immune system and more compassion.[2]

Additionally, there is a surveillance system in our bodies that goes on every minute of our lives, looking for cancer cells in our blood. Because of immune system surveillance, most of the time these cells never congeal and grow to become a problem.

So if the immune system is enhanced through happiness and less stress, it makes sense that cancer might be reduced. Also, genetics may also play a role in cancer longevity. Telomeres are the end part of the chromosome. They protect the chromosome from deterioration. Telomere length is positively associated with longevity. Newer research is demonstrating an increase in telomerase due to compassion training. Telomerase is an enzyme that cleans up broken pieces of DNA, thus lengthening the telomere. So compassion training lengthens telomeres leading to longevity and delayed onset of age-related chronic illnesses. Of course these are complicated subjects and this is still a hypothesis, but studies are ongoing to investigate whether there is any validity to this. [3]

We also need to cultivate respect toward our self. This does not mean promoting the "ego" but rather developing a healthy self-confidence that sees the self as connected with others. In this way healthy self-confidence puts no one down—not our self, nor others. Indeed, such confidence makes it easier to respect others. This also means getting rid of guilt. In the Tibetan language there is no word for guilt. In Buddhism there is no concept of guilt. There are regret and shame. But they don't have those heavy overtones of beating yourself up that guilt does. So there is this Tibetan expression that says: nine times failing, and nine times going forward again. It is very practical. It is learning from your mistakes, but not beating yourself up.

And for those of us who are parents it is very important to love our kids, to really give them affection. It's not enough to feed them and give them pocket money; it's not enough. That robs the child of potential happiness. We need to spend time with them and shower them with affection. We do need some discipline, but children first and foremost need affection. Children who get affection when young are on average happier when they grow up, so don't rob them of their present and future happiness, please.

Next we have to ask, how can we enhance the happiness that we already have? How can we make that happiness richer so that our lives will become more meaningful and the happiness that we have will go out to the world so that the people around us feel it and search for and learn techniques to become happier, themselves.

Happiness is a good thing. We all want to be happy, and none of us want to hurt, but it seems we don't know how to be happy. Generally, the things we look for don't bring us happiness. Choices and higher expectations just make us confused. Pleasure is often confused with happiness. So how do we then find deeper happiness? I don't think there is one simple path to happiness. But there is one avenue that might bring something delightful into our lives, and that is to have a warm heart. Everyone knows how it feels to open your heart. When you have done something for somebody else, you feel good, you feel happy, and it's almost too simple. I think it is really true.

So how can we open our hearts more? How can we become more compassionate and altruistic? One approach that is easy and effective is as follows: Divide all the people and animals in the world into three groups. The first group is those we feel really close to—those we love and care for; usually those same people are kind to us and care for us. They may be family members such as a partner or spouse, a child, a parent, a good friend, or even a teacher. The second group is those who are neutral. We don't know them. You don't know their names or their stories. They are strangers. The third group is those who, in Japan they say are "rubbing your nose." We Americans say, "in your face," or "pushes your buttons." These are people we don't like; people we are not comfortable being around.

If we have the option, we walk the other way and go around to avoid them. I don't want to look at them and I hope they don't see me.

So how do we become happy by looking at people and animals in these three groups?

We focus on seeing kindness shown to us by people from all three groups, choosing a particular individual for the first and third groups. For the second group we reflect on the kindness shown to us by the whole group of strangers since we don't actually know any of them. In that first group it is easy because we usually see that first group of people as kind and connected to us; that is why we love them and feel close to them. We trust them and sometimes depend on them. They are kind to us; they are nice to us. That is not too difficult to see.

With the second group, those we don't know, they are not obviously kind to us. But if we shift our attitude a little bit, reframe our thinking, we can approach our thinking in a fresh way. We can have a very different flavor of this so-called group of neutrals whom we don't know. What we can do is shift our thinking this way: everything that we depend on every day comes from somewhere. For example, earlier today I had a cup of tea. Normally, I don't think about it; I just drink the tea, and if it is good I will have some more. That is one way to approach it. But if I stop and think, where does tea come from? Well, earlier today someone made me a cup of tea, so that person was being very kind, even though I may not know her or him. But where did that person get the tea? She went to the shelf and got a tea bag and boiled some water, but where did the tea bag come from? You start tracing it back and you go back to fields, tea plantations, maybe in India, maybe in China, where people had to till the land. A lot of worms and insects lost their lives in the process. Then the people had to plant the seeds, water and fertilize them. They had to cultivate the land. Then they had to harvest the tea. Near Dharamsala people (usually women) are bent over all day with baskets on their backs picking tea leaves. Then it has to be processed and packaged and then transported. How do all those things happen? Just take the truck that transported the tea from that plantation to the packinghouse. The truck came from a huge factory where many people work, probably thousands, and they all have families. So right away, just drinking one cup of tea involves the hard labor of many individuals and animals. Thus I am so dependent on so many others for everything in my life. This is not just to thrive, but for the bare necessities to survive.

Now, I drink more than one cup of tea a day. I have three meals a day; I have clothing that I wear; I have chairs that I sit in. Or I have books that I want to read that are made from trees, et cetera. I have shelter, a home, and an office, and maybe a car, or two or three. When I am sick I take medicine. Without many of these I simply would not survive. All the electronic things like computers, tablets, smart phones, and other devices that we use are complex and require so many people to produce and acquire. So if we begin to think this way about that second group of people, whom we say we don't really know, we can think, "Wow, this is quite something! They have done all of this for me."

But you might say, "Wait a minute, they didn't do it for me. They don't even know me. They did it because they are making a salary: they have kids to feed, mortgages, gas, and insurance bills to pay. So they didn't intend to do it for me." But no problem, that is right, they are not doing this intentionally for me. Still if they had not made that effort I would not have gotten that cup of tea. I wouldn't have that camera, that clothing, that car or home. So, many people and animals come together to allow me to survive every day, so I don't die but can thrive, enjoy life, and prosper. In that way that whole group of so-called neutral people bring me so much, even if it is unintentional.

For the third group of people, you may say, "Uh oh, no, I don't think so. You are not going to convince me that these people are kind. These guys are my enemies. Whatever I can do to stave them off, that is what I want to do. They show me no kindness; in fact, they show me the opposite."

Is that really true? Well, that is the ordinary way of thinking: Those who make me uncomfortable, I want nothing to do with them; they are just trying to harm me. That is our normal way of thinking, but normally we are not very happy, so maybe our normal way of thinking is limited and narrow-minded. We have the choice to shift our way of thinking to something like this: That third group is in some way being kind to us. How?

We all get angry but anger is an obstacle for us. It doesn't make us feel happy and usually leads to regret and even guilt. We all know how anger destroys our health. It exacerbates high blood pressure leading to heart disease, gives us insomnia, creates stomach ulcers, exacerbates asthma, and on and on. How can we begin to work on our anger, reduce it a bit so we can actually feel happier? When people are in our face, we have an option. We can go with our knee-jerk reaction and get angry and retaliate. Or we can say: "I am not going to react that way. I am going to react with tolerance and patience: I have a choice."

So I am now in this situation. I am getting agitated; I think I am going to get angry and I tell myself I am going to act with patience and tolerance. And then boom, I get angry. It doesn't work the first time. It takes training, like running a marathon—you don't run it after one day of training. The mind is no different. It takes discipline and repeated practice. When I recognize that anger may be around the corner, immediately

I think, "The person I am about to get angry at is not happy." How do I know this? Happy people do not provoke. Therefore, provocative people are not happy. Then I think, "Why is she or he not happy?" Even though I usually don't know the situation, I think of common reasons that set people off. Did he or she exchange some bad words with a girlfriend, boyfriend, a friend, a colleague, or family member? Is she worried about a persistent headache, thinking it might be something serious? Or is he concerned about keeping his job? Just spending thirty seconds or a minute thinking this way leaves no room for my incipient anger to go anywhere. It naturally dissipates. Incipient anger is narcissistic. It demands attention. When we do not pay it attention, it withers on the vine and goes away. Of course this won't work on the first try. We need diligence and persistence; we need to keep trying. Another way to work with early anger is to imagine that it is a cloud far away in the sky. Imagine the cloud drifting across the sky and disappearing along with your anger. Another approach similarly involves imagination. Imagine that your early anger takes on the form of a crystal ball you hold in your hand. Turning your hand over, you drop the imagined crystal ball on a cement surface. The crystal ball shatters in a thousand pieces along with your anger. These practices, when done regularly when anger starts to arise, cultivate a special feeling of closeness toward others, all others. This special feeling of interconnectedness makes it easier to cultivate love and altruism toward others.

In that way, those people who are in our face, making us uncomfortable, these become our teachers because they help us practice patience and tolerance, and they help us become less angry and happier individuals.[4]

It is also important to recognize the relationship between humor, being relaxed, and happiness, which reminds me of the following. There is a doctor whose name is Patch Adams. When he was a resident doctor in West Virginia, on the pediatric rotation taking care of kids with cancer, he would dress up as a clown—big red nose and huge shoes—and he would walk into the children's oncology hospital, and the kids would laugh. They loved it. It didn't matter whether they would soon die, or they would get better, or they wouldn't get better, they always loved it. They felt good. Unfortunately, the hospital administration saw otherwise and he was asked not to come back in a clown's outfit. They made a movie about him, *Patch Adams*, starring Robin Williams, and it brought home this profound truth: humor is very important in helping us feel well. All of us, patients, doctors, and staff alike.

There was an American by the name of Norman Cousins, the editor in chief for the *Saturday Review*. Cousins got sick. All of his joints froze up. He couldn't move, and he was in tremendous pain. So they put him in the hospital. The doctors did all the testing—this, that, and the other. For two weeks they could not decide what the problem was, although Ankylosing Spondylitis was the presumed diagnosis, and they could not treat him adequately. After two weeks in the hospital, he told his good friend, "Get me out of here." He asked his nursing friend to please do three things for him: First, check him out of the hospital and into a hotel; second, hook him up to an IV and give him massive doses of Vitamin C; and third, to please go to the library and check out any book the friend could find on Cousins's favorite humorist, Bennett Cerf. And so the friend did all this and would read Bennett Cerf to him and show him Candid Camera films in the hotel room. Cousins, who could not move and was in tremendous pain, would laugh and laugh and laugh, listening to his favorite humorist. Two weeks later he walked out of the hotel 100 percent cured. It is a true story.

After that UCLA Medical School hired Cousins to be an adjunct professor of medical humanities in the medical school, to teach laughter therapy to the medical students so that they could use it in their practice with people who were hurting. Cousins wrote a book about his experience with intractable illness: *Anatomy of an Illness as Perceived by the Patient: Reflections on Healing.*[5] It was also made into a movie.

Humor is something that is very valuable and makes us feel relaxed. It helps loosen, at least temporarily, the tight grip we have on our ego. This helps us access happiness on a deeper level. The deeper inner happiness is always with us, but emotional ups and downs cloud it. We must come to grips with our negative stuff and work with it. Recognizing our negative emotions and making a commitment to our self to clean them up using emotional hygiene is one important way we access this omnipresent inner happiness.

Chapter 5

Transforming the Negative Emotions: Emotional Hygiene

The Buddha does not wash away negativities with water;
nor does he clear away suffering with his hands;
nor can he transfer his own qualities to you;
he shows the true path;
by that alone are beings liberated.

–The Buddha, *Udanavargavivarana*

I borrow the term "emotional hygiene" from His Holiness the Dalai Lama. It comes from the public health world, where hygiene is a pressing issue. So emotional hygiene is about psychology; it is about the mind. What does this mean? Well, hygiene is about cleanliness, so emotional hygiene is literally the cleaning of the emotions. What does that mean? It means to first recognize our destructive emotions and then constructively transform them into their positive counterparts.

Merely suppressing these destructive emotions does not help, as they hang around and often explode, having become much stronger, later.

Destructive emotions by definition destroy our inner peace. Emotions like anger, jealously, and pride rob us of our peace. So emotional hygiene entails cleaning up those things. Not by suppressing them, because suppressing doesn't work; suppressed emotions just stay, fester, and then boom, some time later they erupt. Emotional hygiene actually transforms these destructive emotions—like churning milk into butter. What happened to the milk? It's transformed into butter. This is the same concept: transforming destructive emotions like anger, jealousy, and pride into their constructive opposites like tolerance, appreciation, and humility. This approach involves recognizing the harmful emotion and then learning and applying the antidote.

We all get angry; it is part of life. We have demands put on us, and we put a lot of demands on ourselves. And we get frustrated; we get irritated, and often that easily leads into anger. So, what do we do about it? Well, first we recognize it. Once anger is full-blown, red hot, we can't do much.

What we try to do is learn to be aware of the early stages of anger. What happens in my body? What happens in my heart? What happens in my mind? What happens in my behavior when I am on that road to getting angry? You have to check up, you have to do your homework. You can't read this in a book, because it is different for every person. There is some commonality, but you have to look inside. So the next time you feel that you are getting angry, examine your feelings. What do they feel like? What is happening inside? What are your thoughts? What are your bodily sensations? Are you reacting to a certain person that you are with? Or to a certain situation, for example, not having slept well last night? So, recognize the situation, and then when you are again in a similar situation start noticing what is happening to you. And then start applying this transformative method.

When we get angry, it is at our self or another person. So let's take the example that we are angry at another person. When this happens to me and I recognize it, right away I think the other person is not happy. Getting angry is a dance involving both parties; both provoke in some way. People that provoke are not happy. I know right away that the other person is not happy. After that I probably don't know much—I may, but often I don't. So I think: relationship problems; health problems; or economic problems? Maybe the person said something unintended to a partner and is feeling bad about it. Or maybe the doctor said, "All your tests are normal except one. Come back and we'll run some more tests." Or maybe the person is worried about keeping his or her job. And just thinking that way takes me maybe fifteen to thirty seconds. What happens to that anger that is starting to come up? It has nowhere to go. It kind of gets lost. Its power and force evaporate. The anger is no longer "coming up" and instead it starts "going down." And in so doing I cause the anger to simply dissolve. Early anger is narcissistic. If it doesn't get the spotlight, it gets bored and goes away.

Now, if you do this once and it doesn't work, you have to do it again and again, because we have had these habits with us, sometimes since childhood. We don't overturn them in a day. It just doesn't work that way. But if you are persistent, this approach will work.

There is another technique taught by Shantideva, the eighth-century Indian Buddhist saint, who wrote the classic book, *A Guide to the Bodhisattva's Way of Life*.[1] He was a student monk at Nalanda University in northeast India, one of the earliest and longest-running universities in the world, dating back to the fifth century CE as a place of learning for about 700 years, until the twelfth century. Shantideva was an embarrassment to the other monks. All they ever saw of him was sleeping, eating, and going to the toilet, which gained him the nickname, Busuku. This means just that—one who eats, sleeps, and goes to the toilet. Every monk during his term at Nalanda University had to make a presentation to the full student body. The tradition was to make a few comments on a classic text. Students had the option to present something original. When it came Shantideva's turn, he chose to present something original. The monks were pleased. They thought he would embarrass himself and thereby hasten his exit from the university. As he gave his original presentation the monks started to listen. When he came to what subsequently became the ninth chapter on wisdom in his *Guide to the Bodhisattva's Way of Life*, Shantideva rose from the throne* and disappeared through the roof. This is the legend. The monks ran after him and apologized, inviting him back to teach. He declined, saying he had other work, but after requests to write down his presentation, he said he had left it in the rafters. His Holiness the Dalai Lama, wherever he travels in the world, takes this book with him. This text is the one he teaches most. Now, back to Shantideva's method to reduce anger.

---

* As a sign of respect when there is an important teaching about enlightenment, the teacher is placed on a raised seat called a throne.

Shantideva asked, if somebody comes and hits us over the head with a stick (or perhaps bad words), why do we get angry with the person? What actually hit our head? A stick. So why don't we get angry with the stick? Many people think that is a ridiculous question, but when you think that way you will begin to chuckle, and then what will happen to the anger? It has nowhere to go; it has been ignored, so it runs away sheepishly and disappears.

So in the case of cutting words, why don't you get angry at the words themselves? The words are the direct, actual culprit that hurt you. So thinking this way we can depersonalize a bit, and Buddhism is all about depersonalizing: reducing attachment, reducing ego. And if we don't have much of an ego, we won't get angry, because there is no one to get angry! And no one to get angry at! And there is no anger! And there is no stick, or no words! Actually our self, the other, the anger, and the stick or words do exist, but not like we think they do.

You may say, "That's not true. Sometimes I am really down on myself, so I don't have much ego and I still get angry at myself." Actually, getting down on oneself is a big ego *trip*, in the sense that it is "me, me, me" stuff. It is self-preoccupation and hence self-cherishing. And that is a big ego, total self-preoccupation. We don't usually think that way but it is more selfish stuff. It is just more self-preoccupation.

Unruly beings are as limitless as space;
they cannot possibly all be overcome.
If I overcome my anger alone,
this will suffice vanquishing all enemies.
—Shantideva, *Bodhisattvachayavatara*

Jealousy can be aggressive like anger, but it is different from anger. Anger is out there. We know when we are angry. It is not hidden. But jealousy is often hiding in the background. We often become jealous without knowing we are jealous. It is usually "off the radar," or subliminal. Jealousy can happen many times in a day without our even knowing it. When we start to take stock and observe what is happening inside us in the present moment (mindfulness), we start to recognize jealousy. Merely recognizing jealousy and exposing it is more than half the battle. Jealousy shuts us down. It closes our heart. It makes us feel contracted and small. Reflecting on the disadvantages of jealousy helps us to get rid of it. When we recognize jealousy and remember its disadvantages, there is no more room for jealousy to grow. It withers on the vine. We begin to appreciate others' good deeds and success. This opens us up. Previously we felt that if someone else is praised or succeeds, in some way this diminishes our own good qualities and reputation. Now we come to know that it is quite the opposite. Being jealous distances us from others, as well as closing our heart. Exchanging jealousy for appreciation opens our heart. Our heart warms, and our chest expands. Naturally a smile brightens the day and we feel well.

Pride is a prison. It is like going to jail and throwing away the key. When we are arrogant we feel as if we know everything. We feel as if we are better than others and know more than they do. Nobody likes being put down, so we lose our friends. We don't trust anybody, and we even become suspicious. We believe we know better than others do. The only thing interesting is boasting of our qualities. Usually this boasting is hot air that no one wants to hear. Before this becomes chronic it is important to wake up and make great effort to get out of this terrible predicament. Remembering the disadvantages of arrogance again and again is helpful. This primes the pump and readies us to dismantle the scaffolding of pride when we are fed up and see beyond the prison. Otherwise we become complacent and lose the energy to change. Then the prison becomes solitary confinement. When we find ourselves being arrogant, it is very important to tell ourselves that this is a trap, that the wall gets too high, and we can't get out. We are stuck. We are lonely and isolated, not a good way to be.

So if we make ourselves vigilantly aware of what is happening inside, right now in the present moment, anger can be transformed into tolerance, understanding, and eventually even compassion. Jealousy can be transformed into appreciation. This is a form of being happy with others' success and good fortune. It is rejoicing in their happiness. Transforming pride into its opposite, humility, is like getting a breath of fresh air. It is like having a death sentence commuted. These transformations are based on recognizing our harmful thoughts and emotions. This is the practice of mindfulness.

Mindfulness

Mindfulness, in the most deeply Buddhist sense of the term, is about a thorough, careful, and calm examination of the contents of our experience. This is an examination that can radically alter our interpretation of that experience by transforming it into its positive opposite. Mindfulness means observing what is happening inside. It means directing a portion of our mind to keep a watchful "eye" on our thoughts and feelings. A portion of the mind acts as a good spy, observing our words and behavior. When this mind, focused inward in the present moment, recognizes a negative intention, thought, or emotion, we have an opportunity to redirect our negative intention to a positive intention. For example, if we notice we are about to tell a lie, or we notice we are actually engaging in telling a lie, then we have the opportunity to stop this deceitful behavior. In this way, we keep track of our words, thoughts, and emotions to ensure they remain honest and positive. When we find we have deviated from being honest and positive, at least we recognize this. Equipped with the understanding of the importance of honesty in maintaining a peaceful, happy life, when we tell a lie or engage in any harmful thought or emotions, we can apologize, tell the truth, and shift to the positive antidote.

So mindfulness used in this way becomes a powerful tool to ensure that we lead our lives in a positive, healthy way. This helps us avoid a negative and unhealthy lifestyle. It gives us the opportunity to reset our course when we have drifted into negative ways of life. I distinguish between two types of mindfulness. One is with a capital M. This is what we are discussing here—an exhaustive, careful, and calm examination of the contents of our human experience, an examination that can radically alter our interpretation of that experience through observing within ourselves our thoughts and emotions in the present moment. Mindfulness with a small m is similar to meditation. This includes both mental concentration training to reduce and eliminate distraction and "monkey-mind," and discursive, or analytical, meditation involving thinking to induce experience. We can investigate compassion, wisdom, tolerance, generosity, and the like. When we induce the feeling of, for example, compassion, we switch to the first type, concentration meditation, and stay with that experience.

There is a definite feeling of well-being when mindfulness is active. We feel more present. Our perspective is vast and wide open. Even when the mindfulness discovers some ill intention, there is calmness. We recognize that we have once again steered onto a wrong path. There is no feeling of guilt, at least after we practice for some time. Rather, there's a sense of steering the boat back onto the course of honesty. There may be some regret, but this is not the same as guilt. We understand that if we were dishonest, we have recognized it and will sincerely try not to repeat it, especially when faced with a similar situation in the future.

In times past, people cultivating honesty and reduction of harmful emotions would remain vigilant. Dipamkara Atisha, an eleventh-century Buddhist master, was invited to Tibet to revive Buddhism. As an old man, he traveled over the Himalayas and then spent his last decade or two in Tibet before he died. He learned Tibetan in order to teach the people there. Wherever he went he watched his own mind with vigilance. When he recognized dishonesty or any destructive emotion, he placed a black stone on a pile. When he recognized honesty or any constructive emotion, he placed a white stone on another pile. Initially the pile with black stones far exceeded the pile with white stones. With practice over time, the proportion gradually shifted, until the white stones exceeded the black ones.

Now back to working with pride and cultivating humility. Sometimes we think humility is a sign of weakness. Some cultures believe this, but some don't at all. I think that our American culture tends in general to see it as a sign of weakness. We like tough guys: Jason Bourne, Dirty Harry, Rambo. But obviously humility is a sign of strength, because it allows us to reduce our ego. And what happens when we reduce our ego?

Love and compassion naturally spring forth. The process is like a teeter-totter. When the ego goes up, love and compassion go down. And vice versa, as our ego comes down and there is more humility, concern for others, love, and compassion go up automatically. Reducing the ego and strengthening our love and compassion require courage. Sometimes I call this the courage of a Samurai spiritual warrior. The enemy is no longer other people. Other people become our dear ones. The enemy becomes that which blocks closeness with them. The enemy becomes the destructive negative emotions, like anger, jealousy, and pride.

> *Give up anger, renounce pride;*
> *overcome all fetters;*
> *cling not to mind and body;*
> *suffering shall never befall you.*
> —The Buddha, *Dhammapada*

Chapter 6

Cultivating Compassion

*If you have not pacified the enemy of your own anger,
combating outer opponents will only make them multiply.
Therefore, with an army of loving kindness and compassion,
to tame your mind is the practice of a Bodhisattva.*

–Gyalsay Thogmay Sangpo, *37 Practices of a Bodhisattva*

Expanding generosity naturally reduces
our self-centered attitude.

Forgiveness comes easier when we distinguish
the person from the person's actions.

Gratitude opens our heart to others.

Fortitude keeps us on track to transform.

Focus and concentration enhance the power
to change positively.

Patience is the strength and courage to discipline
our restraint from harming others.

Wisdom opens the door to reality, hence freedom
(from suffering).

The above essential practices of Buddhism enhance the force of our generosity. When we practice them, there is more power to transform our self-centered ego, which grasps so tightly to our distorted perception of who we are. The resulting detachment is not aloofness. It is the opposite. It brings us closer to others by eliminating the need for continually focusing on me, me, and me. Occasionally when the wisdom feels close and I am able to take a glimpse, the heart feels open and happy. This is not an excited happiness. Rather, it is peaceful with a feeling of vastness. Breathing is easier, fuller, and slower than normal. I feel like I am smiling from deep within myself. Releasing the enormous work of clinging allows for deep relaxation while maintaining alertness.

Generosity

If what we give is likely to be used to harm others, it is better not to give. It is important to take joy in giving. Often we dedicate giving to some higher, altruistic goal. Mentally giving our food, beautiful scenery, delightful sounds of nature and music with a feeling that this imagined gift brings whatever the recipients need to be fully happy makes this meaningful. Then, when I am able to offer everything I encounter that is wholesome toward the enlightenment of everyone, this feels so freeing. Everything seems right and harmonious. This helps ensure that our generosity is not limited due to partiality or bias. Rather, our generosity is directed toward the betterment of humanity and all living beings.

Generosity allows the giver to experience the sympathetic joy of giving to another. It has the potential to direct our positive energy to the welfare of all. Feeling this joy is important. It becomes a strong motivator for us to repeat acts of kindness and charity in the future. The wonderful thing about giving is that it not only benefits the recipient, it also brings profound benefits to the giver. The more one gives, the more one enjoys giving. It seems to snowball for me. When I am in the giving-generous mood, I just want to keep giving. The inner joy is delicious. Mentally giving everything delightful to all living beings has become a habit, especially before I eat. Food tastes better! Of course there is some attachment involved—attachment to the good feeling when giving. Slowly, with practice in reducing the self-grasping to a distorted ego, this attachment will also diminish. Then wisdom motivates our love and compassion. As I said before, self-centeredness and love and compassion are like a balance scale or a teeter-totter. As one goes up the other goes down, and vice versa.

> *Defeat anger by non-anger;*
> *defeat evil by goodness;*
> *defeat stinginess by generosity;*
> *defeat falsehood by truth.*
> –The Buddha, *Dhammapada*

Honesty

Honesty is the foundation of an ethical lifestyle. Without it we are lost. We have no frame of reference out of which we can operate. We lack an ethical compass. Honesty is directed toward others and also directed toward our self. The more honesty we cultivate, especially toward our self, the more we become transparent. Our inner world becomes more congruent with our outer behavior. Honesty and transparency foster respect. Respect is once again both toward others and toward our self. Cultivating respect toward our self makes it easier to respect others. Then it is easier to feel happy rather than become jealous when others experience success and joy. We become gentler with ourselves. This naturally softens us to become gentler with others.

Moreover, this newfound honesty and mutual respect not only soften us and make us gentler, they also cultivate trust. As with honesty and respect, trust is mutual. We find it easier to trust others and be less suspicious. We also find it easier to trust our self. This leads to reduced guilt and a healthier self-confidence. It increases our capacity to spontaneously laugh. We can laugh at our self in a positive way that is nonjudgmental. We are able to genuinely laugh at our self without putting our self down. We become more relaxed and act more naturally. There is less anxiety and fear. Honesty is the foundation for a healthy, balanced, happy life. It is our ethical compass. Without honesty we drift off course, sometimes unknowingly.

Honesty is the foundation for mutual respect. Respect for others moistens our heart with love and compassion. Respect for our self brings healthy self-confidence. Healthy self-confidence gives us the courage and strength to reach out to others. Thus, honesty is the bedrock of compassion. One method of ensuring honesty is mindfulness, discussed in the previous chapter on transforming the negative emotions, what His Holiness the Dalai Lama calls *emotional hygiene*.

Forgiveness

Forgiveness gives us the freedom to let go of hurt. It liberates grudges against others that have been buried, sometimes for a lifetime. Even though the hurt is suppressed, it still keeps a dark cloud over our mood. Forgiveness is the solvent that dissolves the glue that holds our self-righteousness tightly. It softens the

feeling of "I am right and you are wrong. You hurt me." When
I am able to forgive, I recognize the humanity in others. None
of us is perfect. We all make mistakes. We are all deluded. We
are all looking for happiness but we don't know where to find
it. Thus, we harbor many wrong, harmful intentions, thinking
that they are in our best interest.

The harm that has been done to us is of two kinds. It may
have been intentional or unintentional. If the hurt was unintentional, it is easier to forgive. But if the hurt was intentional,
this is more challenging. Yet the fact that the harm was done
intentionally means the other person was not happy. The other
person was out of balance, not in harmony, and likely feeling
hurt her- or himself. Otherwise that person would not have
harmed us. He or she was in the middle of some kind of conflict. It may have been an expression of deep-seated hurt in the
perpetrator, from childhood. Often bullying and abuse arise
from having been bullied or abused. Of course this does not
make it right, but it offers possible understanding.

Happy and balanced people do not go around hurting
others. Recognizing the pain in the one who harms begins to
open our heart to forgiveness. We start to recognize that the
one who harmed was out of control and may well have been
hurt by someone else. Thus, the harm the person caused was
in reaction to something painful he or she received. It was like
a knee-jerk reaction, without much thought. Conflict begets
conflict. In the future, the negative consequences that will
come to the one who harmed, simply as a result of the action
of bringing harm to another, are quite severe. Just thinking
along these lines moistens our heart. It gives us more space,
more breathing room. We feel less closed in and less defensive.
Our sense of retribution lessens. We become more relaxed

and calm. Our fear diminishes. Thus, our heart automatically opens. Forgiveness primarily helps us get rid of pent up hurts. It is much less a matter of right or wrong. The process heals us. More love and compassion begin to flow. Of course, this is a process and takes time. Repeated practice is needed to break our old habits and open our heart more and more.

A wonderful example of the power of forgiveness is told by His Holiness the Dalai Lama.[1] It is a true story about someone he calls his personal hero. This story brings tears to our eyes. Richard Moore was ten years old in 1972 and living in Northern Ireland. A British soldier shot him with rubber bullets, and as a result, Richard became totally blind. The tragedy could have turned the boy into an angry and resentful man. But Richard never bore ill will. Instead he devoted his life to helping and protecting other vulnerable children around the world. He was intent on finding the man who had caused his blindness. When they finally met some time later, Richard told the British soldier that he forgave him. The two men are now friends. This marvelous example of the power of forgiveness is so moving and inspiring.

Patience and Overcoming Anger

Patience is fundamentally the exercise of restraint based on mental discipline. For the most part, it restrains our anger. Essentially, patience is the antidote or counterforce to anger. When we reduce and eliminate our anger, compassion naturally flourishes. As this topic and practice are paramount, I will mention them several times. I hope this will not bore you; I will present the topic from slightly different perspectives. The Tibetan term is *soepa*, which is usually translated as "patience." But it includes the virtues of tolerance, forbearance, and forgiveness. Its deeper meaning is the ability to endure suffering. It implies not giving in to our instinctive urge to reflexively respond to our pain in harmful ways. But soepa has nothing to do with being passive or impotent. It does not mean lacking the strength or ability to fight back with the courage of compassion. Nor is it gritting our teeth and enduring injustice grudgingly. Instead, genuine patience requires strength and courage. Strength and mental courage are required to discipline the mind. Mental discipline helps us to restrain harmful ways of living, particularly anger. Standing up to injustice becomes natural. No longer is aggression the means. As a Samurai spiritual warrior, we fight with love and compassion for all parties, both victim and perpetrator. We fight the enemy, destructive emotions. We realize the pain of the victim as well as the future painful consequences to the perpetrator.

Patience interrupts our automatic tendency to take revenge through anger. Mental discipline requires that we adopt a wider, more holistic view. Adopting a wider, panoramic perspective gives us an understanding of the complete situation. This allows us the emotional space to distance our self from the feelings of anger. Having emotional space, we are no longer boxed into an emotional corner. We learn how to avoid identifying with the anger. When we train in recognizing anger early, we can just let the feeling of anger go without clutching onto it as ours. We simply imagine the anger floating away like a cloud drifting naturally across the sky. By not tightly identifying with the anger, we are able to let it go. With this visualization comes a distance and space between our self and our anger. Thus, with this space it becomes easier to separate from the anger. Therefore, we have more room to relax. We have let go of identifying the anger as "me" or "mine." Here it is helpful to make a distinction between the person and the action. It allows us to have tolerance and forgiveness toward the person, yet still be opposed to the action. Very harmful actions may need appropriate punishment according to the law. Of course, it is the person who committed those actions that is punished. Yet still we maintain our respect and compassion for the person who caused the harm. For given the right circumstances it could have been us.

We are all human, and as humans we make mistakes. At the same time, we all have this amazing potential to become better human beings. We all have this precious Buddha nature to become totally pure. This is what we respect within the perpetrator and within all living beings. The perpetrator has the potential to turn his or her life around and become a better human being.

In order to overturn anger, it is important to reflect on its disadvantages. This helps us to strengthen our resolve to practice patience. Intense moments of anger create tremendous difficulties for us later on. They delete our history of wholesome actions. Thus, the beneficial, happy results from doing good are no longer available to us. Anger also has insidious, corrosive effects on our mood and on our present state of happiness. Steadily repeated anger gradually undermines our inner peace. It deprives us of our clarity. We lose the panoramic view. Hence, decision making becomes clouded and takes on a narrow scope. Anger hinders our altruistic nature, which is the source of our greatest happiness. In fact, it would be fair to say that all the violence and destruction in the world is the result of aggression based on anger and hatred, which is often based on attachment.

The damaging consequences of anger and hatred can be seen clearly in domestic violence. They are also the sources of communal violence and war. Anger often arises out of a deeper, inner dissatisfaction. This latent state of irritability and a lack of contentment is called *mi dewa* in Tibetan. It is a general underlying state of unease, setting a tone, or as Dr. Paul Ekman would say, a mood, that underlies flares of angry emotion.[2]

This discontent makes us more susceptible to triggering destructive emotions, especially anger. Dissatisfaction in our life is the fuel that sparks the fire of destructive emotions such as anger, hostility, and hatred. Therefore, just as recognizing sparks before the fire can prevent the fire, similarly recognizing an underlying mood of discontent can modulate the expression of anger. When we start to see things from this new perspective, we begin to recognize that these destructive emotions feed upon themselves. The more they are indulged, the more they intensify. To address such self-perpetuating destructive emotions, it is helpful to turn our attention inward. We become more familiar with our tendencies and habits. Instead of blaming others and the world, we become more mature by identifying patterns of emotions and behavior, and work on our self.

The great eighth-century Buddhist master Shantideva makes this point exceedingly well when discussing how to manage anger.[3] If we wish to prevent our feet from being pricked by thorns, it would be foolish to try covering the whole world with leather. Rather, it would be much more reasonable to cover just the soles of our feet. In the same way, it is a mistake to think we will get rid of anger by changing everything and everyone around us. Instead it would be much better to change our self.

> *Where could I possibly find enough leather*
> *with which to cover the surface of the earth?*
> *But wearing leather the size of the soles of my shoes,*
> *Suffices covering the entire earth.*
> –Shantideva, *Bodhisattvachayavatara*

Compassion as a way of life naturally condemns wrong actions and opposes them with all means necessary, while at the same time maintaining respect for the person engaged in the harmful actions. Forgiveness does not mean ignoring or forgetting. Instead, it is a way of dealing with wrongdoing that brings peace of mind. At the same time, it prevents us from succumbing to the harmful impulses of revenge. By distinguishing the deed from the person performing the deed and by understanding the situation in its entirety, we come to the conclusion that the person who harmed us also deserves our compassion. Severe, painful consequences of the person's harmful actions await that person in the future. Of course, thinking from this perspective is not easy, so we practice step by step. Practicing patience and forgiveness repeatedly is enormously liberating for us. I remember my feelings when hearing the story of the Irish boy, Richard Moore, who was shot with rubber bullets.

When we dwell on the harm someone has done to us, we become angry and resentful. When we practice forgiveness and compassion, we let go of anger and resentment. Clinging to painful memories and harboring ill will cannot reverse the wrongs done to us. Such an approach does not help. On the contrary, our peace of mind is disturbed and we do not sleep well. Our immune system weakens and eventually our physical health declines.[4] We develop more heart problems and suffer more accidents. If, on the other hand, we are able to overcome our feelings of hostility toward those who harm us and forgive them, there is immediate and perceptible benefit. It is not at all necessary to tell the other person of our forgiveness, though of course we can if we like. The practice of forgiveness allows us to breathe easier and become more relaxed, with blossoming inner peace and confidence. This is my experience. It feels like a heavy weight has been lifted from my shoulders. My body feels lighter, and the whole world looks brighter. I have the feeling that I can now move on and get on with my life.

Perseverance, Enthusiasm, and Joyous Effort

Perseverance means not giving up, even in the face of adversity. It means not allowing our tendencies toward laziness and procrastination to control our lives. It is digging in our heals. A new courage that confidently says, "I can do it" is nurtured. With this confidence comes a new sense of meaning and purpose. It is not just continuing our efforts out of boredom and drudgery. Rather, there is an enthusiasm born of understanding the long-term benefits of not giving up when doing good things. We gain a sense of conviction in the long-term benefits of what we are trying to do. Perseverance reduces our lazy tendency of giving up, especially when we are working for the higher purpose of concern for others. It gives us more confidence that we can succeed. What higher purpose could there be than working for the welfare of others?

There are two kinds of benefits. There is the benefit that comes to the other and the benefit that comes to us. We feel relaxed and happy, gaining a new sense of meaning in our life. This brings more fulfillment, satisfaction, and contentment. Money cannot buy these things. When I persevere in the face of obstacles and finally complete the wholesome task at hand, I feel very satisfied, regardless of the outcome. There is a sense of achievement and long-term meaning. Doing wholesome things makes me feel *well* and good inside. The Tibetan word for "perseverance," *tsondu* (brtson-'grus), actually has a joyous quality to it, not a feeling of drudgery. There is also a sense of enthusiasm that comes from knowing that what we are doing is worthwhile.

Concentration

In order to practice generosity, forgiveness, patience, persever-ance, and all the wholesome qualities successfully, we need a focused, nondistracted mind. Focused attention, or concen-tration, breaks the habit of distraction. Additionally, it brings more clarity and brightness to the mind. It interrupts rumi-nation. It interrupts multitasking. It interrupts that incessant internal chatter, thereby allowing us to channel our energies in a healthy direction. In this way, the mind and heart become more stable and clear. The mind and heart become more powerful, like a laser. In this way, as we utilize this laser-like mind, decisions become clearer and more effective. The mind gains a wider perspective through concentration, by reducing the "noise." Potential distractions are shut out. The situation at hand becomes crystal clear, as there are no distractions to cloud the mind. Hence, the mind is more relaxed. We become calmer, as there is less clutter. The mind no longer jumps around like a monkey. This creates a spaciousness and openness in the mind and heart. Within this open space, there is distance from unwanted thoughts and emotions. We are more able to sepa-rate from these thoughts and emotions. Thus, we have more freedom of choice to engage or not engage with these thoughts and emotions. The mind and heart can investigate multiple scenarios efficiently, moving smoothly and with ease; decision making has more breadth and more effectiveness, powered by efficiency.

When my mind is concentrated, I feel very alert and relaxed and am able to see things from a broad perspective. Making decisions becomes easy. There is no anxiety or fear. I seem to have greater vision. I feel more at peace. There is balance between alertness and relaxation. The cultivation of concentration is a process, and I have not achieved the full degree of concentration; yet when my mind is somewhat concentrated, I feel totally absorbed. Time is absent.

When I arise from a concentration meditation I am surprised by how much time has passed. It has seemed like five minutes, yet the clock says thirty. My body feels very light and I feel as if I do not need to sleep. Of course, this doesn't happen often and later I get tired and sleep. My sleep is often deep and undisturbed when I am on a meditation retreat. There is a feeling of peace and deep relaxation. When I remember the Buddhist wisdom, my mind sometimes goes deeper. It becomes subtler and spacious. Alternate methods of cultivating compassion, such as generosity, forgiveness, patience, and concentration become powerful tools even when we are practicing compassion directly. They moisten the heart and reduce our pride, anger, jealousy, and selfishness. Many avenues lead to the same result. Walking them all strengthens our altruism and makes us happier.

Chapter 7

Insight

We do not say that because things are empty they do not exist;
we say that because things exist they are empty.

—A Prasangika-Madhyamaka Tibetan Saying

In an earlier chapter, I spoke in terms of Buddhist wisdom in understanding the nature of reality. The Buddha taught us there are two aspects of reality, which he called "Two Truths." The Buddha, Nagarjuna, Shantideva, and other Buddhist scholar-saints have begun the discussion on insight or wisdom by explaining the two truths. Understanding them both helps us avoid the two extremes. First, let me explain the two truths, the two extremes, and finally how the two truths protect us from falling into the two philosophical extremes of reality.

The two truths are conventional truth and ultimate truth. Ultimate truth is emptiness. We arrive at the ultimate truth, that is, understanding emptiness, through analysis. Proper analysis helps us gain understanding and then conviction. Once conviction in the ultimate truth of emptiness is gained through study and contemplation, we can take it deeper through meditation. The central argument, or logic, that is used is the argument of "sameness or difference." In this approach we analyze anything (i.e. phenomenon) with respect to its parts, or basis, analyzing whether the thing is identical to its parts or completely different or separate from them. The more we do this analysis, the more we realize that the thing we are analyzing is neither identical to nor different from its parts. As there is no third alternative, slowly we come to the realization the thing cannot exist. What we are analyzing is the normal appearance of that thing; the normal appearance of anything is that it exists from its own side. This is the same as existing objectively or independently, and not depending on a perceiving mind to observe it. Taking this approach into meditation, first we analyze in the same manner. This is contemplative, or analytical, meditation. When we gain conviction in the "unfindability" of the thing, then we shift to concentration meditation. We concentrate on that unfindability. The more we search, the less able we are to find that thing. We concentrate solely on the absence of that thing. Thus, while one is meditating on emptiness, nothing appears before the mind. In this way we become, or merge with emptiness. This is contemplative meditation where we become one with the object of meditation, in this case emptiness. But this does not mean that nothing exists. It means the distorted appearance (the normal appearance) of that thing does not exist. Still that thing exists, someone meditating exists, but not the way they appear. So from the perspective of things existing but not as they appear, we are now talking about a subtler understanding of conventional truth or reality, the second of the two truths. As our understanding and realization of emptiness deepens through meditation, so does our understanding of conventional truth or reality. After we meditate a long time on emptiness, when we arise from our meditation everything appears illusory, like a dream. We see and hear things but we are convinced they are not real. We are convinced they are like illusions. Conventional truth is also referred to as truth for the concealer, or veiled truth. This suggests the almost illusory experience following meditation on emptiness. Things appear as before, but we are convinced they do not exist in that same way. Hence they are like illusions: they are concealed; they are veiled. The important point here is that the deeper our understanding of the ultimate truth of emptiness, the deeper is our understanding of conventional truth.

The two extremes of reality are nihilism and reification. Reification is inflating reality. It is making more of something than is actually there. It is objectifying. Conventional truth protects us from nihilism, the belief that nothing exists. Ultimate truth protects us from reification, believing more exists than is actually there. It is an emptiness or absence of mistaken appearances. It is an absence of reification or objectifying. Conventional truth protects us from negating reality altogether. Conventional truth is the means that allows us to investigate reality or emptiness. Emptiness allows a changing reality, that is, conventional reality. So ultimate truth and conventional truth are mutually supportive. Actually they have the same meaning, but are expressed differently. So now you may have a glimpse of why the Buddha began his teachings on wisdom or insight with the presentation of the two truths. These two truths are ubiquitous. They apply to everything. They are qualities of everything that exists.

Let's take an example, "my self." Now the parts, or basis, of my self are my body and my mind. Further elaborated, there are the five aggregates: form (or the physical body) and four different aspects of mind or consciousness. In Buddhism "mind" and "consciousness" are synonymous. They both refer to thoughts, feelings, emotions, and all mental states. This includes all experience. So we start the inquiry comparing these two: my self on one hand, and my body and mind on the other. First we ask and consider: Are they exactly the same, identical? If they are, the name "my self" is redundant. Also the name "my self" makes no sense, as it would be fully expressed in "my body and my mind." Furthermore, when my body dies, then "my self" should die. But we know from Buddhism and other Eastern philosophies that the self continues from life to life as the continuity of the subtle mind. The other possibility is that "my self" and the basis, or parts, my body and my mind, are totally different and separate. But this is very strange. We often say, "my body" or "my mind." Also, actions done by "my self" could never ripen on my body or mind. Conversely, results of actions ripening on me could not have been performed by my body or my mind. These contradictions begin to erode our conviction in an objective self. "My self" or "I" becomes elusive. After searching extensively many times, we cannot find "my self" either as identical or different from my body and mind. As there is no third alternative, slowly we come to the conclusion that "my self" cannot be found. If it cannot be found after extensive repeated searching, we come to the conclusion that it does not exist.[1]

When we look deeper into the nature of anything—our self (our ego), our body, our mind, the chair we are sitting on, the table in front of us—when we look deeper we actually can't find anything. We rest in this unfindability in meditation. At first this "loss" may bring discomfort or even fear. Gradually, the fear of losing our self gives way to an utter joy, an utter peace and happiness. For this is the true nature of reality, unfabricated and peaceful. This is freedom.

Conventional truth is our everyday, common experience of the world of things, experienced as "objective reality." It makes sense to our senses because they are under the influence of ignorance, and it is reinforced by our language, with its emphasis on the structure of subject, object, and action or verb. All of this experience with conventional truth leads us to think that this is simply the way things are. But Buddhist reflection on the deeper aspects of life and existence leads to a different way of understanding and experiencing the world.

So, when you go deeper into investigating reality, particularly our self—who we are—what we find is that when we come out of that meditation and we reflect on our self, we see our self as like an image in a dream when we wake up, kind of like an illusion. The Buddha taught that everything is like a dream, like an image in a dream upon waking. You wake up, and you have had a dream of a good friend and you feel very happy. It is almost as if your friend is still there. And then the feeling dissipates and goes away and you say it was only a dream. The Buddha said that when you wake up to reality it is like that. Everything you see, you recognize as false, just like an image in a dream upon awakening.

The Buddha also said everything is like a mirage, like water in a mirage as we go closer. He also taught that everything is like a reflection, like a reflection of the moon in still water or the reflection of a face in a mirror. We take that reflection to be our actual face. You look in the mirror and you start primping; you put on your makeup and comb your hair, and you check in the mirror. Does it look good, does it not look good? Am I beautiful? Am I ugly? Change the hair a little bit as if that face I am looking at in the mirror were really my face. But it is not, it is only a reflection. We forget that. This points to the Buddhist wisdom. The Buddha taught these analogies to explain conventional reality—things appear one way but exist in another way.

The Buddha taught these three analogies and others to explain reality. These analogies allow us to realize the illusory nature of reality. When you wake up from ignorance it is the same kind of feeling as when you wake up from a dream. Things appear one way, but they actually exist in another way. It is the same type of feeling of seeing through falsity, but with a tremendous difference in perspective, feeling, and intensity. This awakening from ignorance is a little like quantum physicists searching for subatomic particles. The more they search, the less clear these so-called particles are. They come to the conclusion that particles do not exist objectively. They see through the falsity of objective particles or objective reality. This process could be seen as a massive black hole "eating" all of our ignorance, leaving only the tremendous light of the event horizon with its escaping invisible x-rays, radio waves, and invisible gases filled with unconditional love and joy. This could be in a textbook on quantum physics, although it is only a rough analogy.

Raja Ramanan was a great Indian physicist, sometimes called the father of nuclear energy in India. And he informed the Dalai Lama some years back that the concept of no objective reality existed in India two thousand years ago. He had read the writings of Nagarjuna, who is like the second Buddha and who lived two thousand years ago, and he knew from his reading that the principles were very similar to modern quantum physics. Let me explain a little about Nagarjuna's magnum opus, *Fundamental Verses on the Middle Way*. This explanation is based on my forthcoming book in press, *Nagarjuna's Wisdom: A Guide to Practice*.[2]

Nagarjuna's six extant compositions are masterpieces in understanding the *prajnaparamita* (perfection of wisdom) teachings of the Buddha. His *Fundamental Verses on the Middle Way*[3] may be the quintessential classic Buddhist text on understanding Madhyamaka, or the middle way philosophy, explaining who we are deeply, and what the world is deeply. Nagarjuna was prophesized by the Buddha and lived almost 2000 years ago. He is probably the greatest scholar and practitioner after the Buddha. Nagarjuna was a professor at Nalanda Monastic University in northern India, one of the biggest and longest-running universities, teaching monastic students from the fifth to the twelfth centuries. His work is relatively terse, often written in four-line verse form. Nagarjuna attempts to thoroughly explain the most difficult teachings of the Buddha—*Sunyata* in Sanskrit, or *emptiness* in English. He uses reasoning and logic extensively. His four-pointed logic—tetralemma—is famous, especially as applied to the production of all phenomena. This means how everything comes into existence or is born. All things and events appear to be objective. So Nagarjuna is investigating whether objective things can exist. These are the only four possibilities of how all (objective) things could come in to existence. By extensively refuting all four possibilities, Nagarjuna concludes that things are not produced objectively or intrinsically. He writes that things are produced neither from themselves, nor from others, nor from both, nor from neither (causelessly).

Nagarjuna's writings are not easy to understand and require much effort and persistence to unpack. There have been many attempts to explain his words in the form of commentaries over the centuries. One of Nagarjuna's main disciples Candra-kirti, wrote two main commentaries on Nagarjuna's *Wisdom*. One is called, *Entering the Middle Way*. It attempts to explain the meaning of Nagarjuna's verses. The other is *Clear Words*, which attempts to explain Nagarjuna line-by-line and word-by-word. Another main disciple of Nagarjuna is Aryadeva. He also wrote a classic commentary on Nagarjuna's *Wisdom*.

Many centuries later, in the latter part of the fourteenth century, Je Tsongkhapa wrote *Ocean of Reasoning*, a further commentary on Nagarjuna's *Wisdom*.[4] About four hundred years ago the first Dalai Lama, Gendun Drup, also wrote a clear commentary. Each of these classic commentaries has spurred many other commentaries trying merely to understand the original commentary. So you see this is not easy stuff. Nevertheless, it is quintessential if we genuinely want to free ourselves and everyone else from ingrained distorted ignorance toward our ego and the world, which brings about relentless suffering. For this is the only way to find unconditional inner peace and happiness. So we'll give it a shot!

Nagarjuna opens his book with an oft-quoted salutation:

I praise that Perfect Buddha,
The best of all Teachers,
Who taught us dependent origination,
Free of cessation and production,
Without disintegration and permanence,
With no coming and no going,
Neither same nor different,
The quieting of all fabrications,
The supreme bliss.

Nagarjuna is summarizing all that exists as dependent arisings, and characterizing them in four pairs—production and cessation, permanence and disintegration, coming and going, and sameness and difference. This characterizes things being born and dying, things lasting and not lasting, things in motion, and things' identities either isolated or relational. All of these aspects of reality are dependent and relational, not objective and independent. This is a powerful way to start a text. It sets the stage for this overarching, ubiquitous understanding of reality that nothing exists intrinsically or objectively.

In *Fundamental Wisdom* and other treatises, Nagarjuna uses the logic of *reductio ad absurdum*, as well as other forms of logic, to question ordinary perceptions and conceptions that things exist truly. This type of logic reduces the opponents' arguments to a tangle of contradictions. In the first verse of chapter one Nagarjuna writes:

> *Neither from itself nor from another,*
> *nor from both nor without a cause*
> *is anything, anywhere, at any time,*
> *ever produced. (1:1)*

Some scholars, both old and new, have interpreted this verse to mean that Nagarjuna is a nihilist. However, this is short-sighted. For Nagarjuna demonstrates that things do indeed exist, but not intrinsically. They exist dependently, nominally as designations, as he expressed in chapter 24:

> *Whatever is dependently originated,*
> *is explained to be emptiness.*
> *That, being a dependent designation,*
> *is itself the middle way. (24:18)*

> *There does not exist anything*
> *that is not dependently originated.*
> *Therefore there does not exist*
> *anything that is not empty. (24:19)*

Nagarjuna articulated and defended the philosophical view of emptiness like a fierce warrior. But he did not stop there. He also taught the most precious practice of *Bodhicitta*, which explains emptiness and unconditional compassion as the path to enlightenment. So we practice this path in order to guide all others to that same enlightened state. This is how we can be of maximal benefit to others. Nagarjuna writes, in his *Precious Garland of Advise for a King (Ratnāvalī)*:

> *May I be beloved of beings, and may they*
> *be more beloved to me that myself.*
> *May I bear the results of their negativity,*
> *and may they have the results of all my virtue.*

> *As long as there is even a single*
> *sentient being anywhere who is not yet free,*
> *may I remain in the world for that being's sake,*
> *even if I have attained unexcelled awakening.* (5:84–85)

These verses are the foundation for the cultivation of the practice of exchanging the attitude of cherishing oneself for the attitude of cherishing others. This exchange culminates in Bodhicitta. These two verses, 5:84 and 5:85 from Nagarjuna's *Precious Garland*, are the culmination of his twenty verses arousing Bodhicitta.

Let's return to quantum physics and its relationship to the philosophy of the Buddha and Nagarjuna. Albert Einstein's special and general theories of relativity painted a similar picture of reality, the opposite of the idea that we generally buy into, of the existence of something objective and solid. Einstein's special theory of relativity says there is no absolute frame of reference.

So I want to look at this question of there being no objective reality by examining some fascinating correspondences between Buddhist teachings and quantum physics. What I have come to understand, though not fully, is that quantum physics' approach to understanding micro reality is very apropos to understanding our minds, our hearts, and in fact all of reality.

The physicist David Bohm was a very close friend of the Dalai Lama. Bohm said that there is no objective reality. What does it mean that there is no objective reality? Bohm did not say that there was nothing, rather that there were only events and processes, so that everything must be seen in terms of relationship. Everything is changing. There are no solid, independent things like the ones we normally view, either worldly phenomena or our egos.

So, what was the genesis of Bohm's radical shift in thinking? As David Darling explains, at the end of the nineteenth century, classical Newtonian science, which assumed that there was objective reality and that consciousness had no special relevance to understanding the world, was in serious trouble.[5] As physicists began looking into the subatomic world, it became clear that there was an intimate connection between the mind of conscious observers and that which was being observed. One way of understanding this subatomic world was by observing the properties of radiation waves given off when matter was heated, demonstrating the equivalence of matter and energy. This understanding of the equivalence of matter and energy began to break down the notion of a solid, fixed world.

In short, the conclusion of quantum experimentation was that it was no longer meaningful to think of an electron (as an element of matter) as always being definitely somewhere or "somewhen" when it was not being observed. Indeed, "it could not be claimed, in the new quantum picture of the world, that particles even truly *exist* outside of our observations of them. They have no independent, enduring reality in the familiar classical sense of being like tiny beads of matter with a definite ... location in space and time."[6]

Such a concept was later demonstrated by the double-slit experiment, in which electrons were fired one at a time through an interference barrier with two slits and were registered on a photographic plate. When one slit was open, each electron made an imprint on the plate as a particle. However, when two slits were open and a large number of electrons were fired, the imprint left on the plate showed that the electrons passed through both slits simultaneously, indicating a wave-like pattern. Thus electrons could be viewed as either wave or particle, depending on whether or not they were observed, which meant that the nature of reality was determined by observation.

In other words, just as Newtonian physics continues to adequately explain the world at the macro level of physics, it does not effectively explain the more subtle aspects of reality at the subatomic level. This understanding could also be a textbook on Buddhist philosophy, which reminds us to realize the gap between appearance (usual understanding) and reality (deeper understanding). What we hear, see, and think, we take it as real. There is a real, objective referent out there. I am thinking about the computer on which I am writing this book—well, I just make the assumption that there is a real, solid screen there. But when we recognize the gap, we start to look more deeply at the appearances in our mind and we begin to realize that there is no real referent out there. Similarly there is no real referent in there, in our mind. And that's just what David Bohm was talking about.

Chapter 8

Approaching Death and Dying without Fear

Collections in the end disperse;
whatever rises must also fall;
and meetings end in separation;
the final end of life is death.
–The Buddha—*Dhammapada*

I want to focus on approaching death without fear. I want to state clearly that to understand death we must come to recognize that death is a part of life. Not as a cliché but actually a part of life. This also means to recognize that we have done this many times before. And very likely we will do this many times again.

It takes some of the burden off us when thinking about our own death if we recognize that this is not the absolute end. Now, that statement has a proviso. And the proviso is this: *that we have led a reasonably good life, have been a reasonably good person, and have not engaged in repeated harm to others.* This is an important proviso because of this basic truth: our actions follow us. Our actions may be finished but there is some residual that stays, and that residual element determines our experience in the next moment and in the next life. If we are someone whose life has been guided by the actions of helping and not harming, our experience in that next moment will be a pleasant one. We will feel well. And the opposite holds true: If we have lived a life of harming others, our next experience after our last breath will not be so pleasant. So the proviso here is that we have been reasonably good in avoiding causing harm.

Let's get into how Buddhist teachings approach death and dying.

A monk meditating on corpses at different stages of decomposition, a practice that brings awareness of one's own mortality and impermanence.

There is a Buddhist practice discussed in an ancient Buddhist text *The Four Foundations of Mindfulness* that is especially prominent in parts of Southeast Asia, such as Thailand, Burma, Laos, Cambodia, and Sri Lanka. Here the monks will view corpses at different stages of decomposition. They do this to become familiar with the fact that we are actually going to die, even me. We come to see that our bodies are "full of various kinds of unclean things," and the writings of the great masters instruct us to meditate on such bodily ingredients as "feces, bile, phlegm, pus, blood, sweat, fat, tears, skin-oil, saliva, mucus, fluid in the joints, urine, etc." It also calls for us to imagine our bodies "one day, two days, three days dead—bloated, livid, and festering." Through this practice we realize the body is filthy, helping us to reduce attachment. We further realize our mortality, that indeed we will die. And death may come at any moment. This is true not only for us, but for everyone. The practice of love and compassion becomes paramount.

In our modern world we have forgotten a number of important points about life and death:

- We have forgotten that death is natural.
- We have forgotten that in the days of our grandparents, people died at home with the whole family witnessing the process.
- This cultivated some familiarity with death, reducing our fear.
- Today, most people die in hospitals, often not seen by family and friends. And death often happens late at night or early in the morning, when family may not be around.

This distancing from death, this cultural and medical development, makes death more of a mystery and something unknown. And it is just this distancing from death that allows for more fear to arise around death. We fear what we don't know and understand. In those not-so-distant times, when death was a family affair taking place in the home, the dying person was surrounded by family members providing comfort.

Now, Buddhists meditate on death regularly, and they do not do it to become depressed over a sad fact of life. They do it because awareness of death becomes a stimulus. When we recognize our inevitable death, this recognition stimulates us to do what is important now. Not to procrastinate so much. It helps us remain aware that we are mortal.

The time of our death is uncertain. Many of us think, "Okay, I'm 60, I've got 20 years," or "I'm 100, I've got 10 years." Recently I met a wonderful lady who is 104. She is a nun of the Order of St. Francis and lives in Minnesota. She has long, flowing red hair, and in her order most nuns do not wear typical nun habits, but regular dress. I was invited to a pre-Lent Mardi Gras party with this lively community. They invited some musicians to play. They had two punches: one clean and one spiked. Some of the nuns were sipping the spiked punch. As a monk I don't drink alcohol. And then we danced. Vera, who only three months prior had the need to start using a walker, tossed her walker aside and started dancing. So maybe for her she is thinking at 104 that she will live another ten years. Maybe she will. This seems possible, particularly when we consider the amazing humanitarian work these elderly nuns are engaged in. They are fiercely fighting human trafficking right there in their own community. They are teaching love and compassion not as a passive way to live, but rather as an active way to fight injustice without anger.

So the time of our death is uncertain. We know people who have died young, when they were children or young adults. No one knows when they will die. So to get the important things done now is something that comes out of this regular contemplation about our own death.

Shakespeare wisely puts it this way in *The Tempest* (with my Buddhist interpretations in brackets):

. . . our actors all melted into air. . .
[impermanence—everyone is going to die]
all that is inherited shall dissolve . . .
[even the hard stuff: Our possessions, our loved ones, our
bodies will not help us at the time of our death—they all
must be left behind.]
this insubstantial pageant faded
[everything goes: our palaces, our high rises, nothing stays
forever]
Leaves not a rack [trace] behind
[so is completely gone]
we are such stuff as dreams are made of . . .
[insubstantial, like illusions, not real]

Above I spoke of two benefits of the Buddhist practice of meditating on death (less procrastination, stimulus to do the important things now). Now I want to mention two more benefits:

- ◆ When we die, we will have less regret because we have taken care of the meaningful and important things in life. We have not lived lives in which we pushed important aspects of living under the rug.
- ◆ We will have less fear. This is a profound truth. You can see this with people who are dying who have reached a stage where they feel they have done the things they need to do; they can die in peace.

Now let's turn to what happens when we go through the death process.

Embryology

I want to turn to embryology, because I'm a doctor. So, we have conception, in which sperm and egg unite. From a Buddhist perspective, the mind, or consciousness, also unites at conception. This is the continuity of mind, or stream of consciousness, that enters to create a new life at conception. As the fetus develops, many, many changes take place. Cells divide, then rudimentary appendages and organs develop into what we can term the gross physical body. What most of us didn't learn about embryology, particularly not in medical school, is that when the sperm, egg, and mind/consciousness come together, we then have a different kind of embryology, which is in tandem or parallel with the development of the gross physical body. This different embryology involves what is called the "subtle body." The subtle body is made up of channels, chakras, and essences. In Tibetan we call this *tsa lung tigle*. This knowledge comes from adepts who meditate on the channels, chakras, and essences flowing within, particularly the changes that come about as a result of these practices, which radically alter their human experience, bringing joy, insight, and love.

In Buddhism, we recognize an embryology of the subtle body system. This system begins when the sperm, the egg, and the mind unite. And it begins at what will become the heart chakra—the center of the body, in the center of the area that will become the child's chest, between the breasts and in front of the backbone. This happens early on, just after conception. What happens during the early embryology of the subtle body is that that point at the center of the chest, which will later form the heart chakra, first elongates north and south vertically, forming what we call the central channel. It is thin, maybe the thickness of a thin straw; it is made of energy; and it is translucent, with a bluish hue. It is not gross, hard physical stuff. When surgeons open up the chest, they don't see these things. But when you talk to meditators who have been meditating on these things for years, they will tell you these things absolutely do vividly exist in their imagination and experience; and not only that, by meditating on these chakras, they can bring about powerful changes in their lives that bring incredible joy, unimaginable love and compassion, and the most profound wisdom. They create powerful consequences and unimaginable results through this meditation.

The heart chakra is an outgrowth from the central channel, as are all the six chakras. This number varies a bit in different Vajrayana (Tantra) systems, but the standard system contains five or six chakras (depending whether you include the forehead, "third eye" chakra). But what happens next is that at the five or six places, the central channel starts to branch, becoming the chakras—at the forehead; the crown; the throat; the heart; four finger widths below the navel; then at the secret place, the tip of the sexual organs of both men and women. These places are chakras, and from this central channel, in each of these places branches develop that come out in four directions: front, back, right, and left. So four branches come out from the central channel at the level of each of the chakras. Then each of those branches bifurcates again into two, which continues, forming each chakra. Thus each chakra contains anywhere from eight to sixty-four branches. At the crown chakra, there are thirty-two branches. At the throat chakra there are sixteen. At the heart chakra there are eight. At the navel chakra there sixty-four. And at the secret sexual organ there are thirty-two branches.

Now, at each chakra the right and left branch move laterally, perforating the parallel right and left channels that run along the sides of the central channel [Fig. 1]. In this way a communication is formed between the central channel and the side channels that communicate with all the other channels. In addition, the right and left channels loop around the central channel at the level of each chakra, causing constriction [Fig. 2]. At the heart chakra, the constriction is greatest as each of the right and left channels wraps around three times (a total of six constrictions). This, under normal circumstances, constricts the flow of energy into the central channel. So under normal circumstances, the central channel is flat, without any flow of energy. Our job as meditators is to reverse the flow and fill the central channel with the vital essence of energy. This is done by releasing the constricting right and left channel loops at the level of each chakra, through continual meditation focusing the mind at these vital points. This requires concentration and visualization of the chakra. Gradually, the constrictions loosen, allowing the vital energy to flow within the central channel. Causing the vital energy to melt and flow within the central channel is achieved by activating, through meditation, a small flame at the navel chakra, which begins the flow of energies within the central channel. This meditation is called kundalini in Hindu traditions. The Buddhist practice was adapted from the ancient Indian systems. In Tibetan this meditation practice is called *tummo*. The practices of Bodhicitta and Sunyata were added to make a more complete practice situated within universal compassion, embedded in the ground of reality—the reality of emptiness. The white essence melts from above and the red essence from below. Great bliss and unconditional love result, all bathed in the most profound wisdom of realizing reality directly, without any conceptual intermediary, exactly as it is.

In the chakra diagram, there is a hole in the middle of the branches. That is the central channel as seen from above, looking down [Fig. 3]. Imagine the channel coming out at you. It goes vertical in front of the spine. Remember that the chakra is branching out from the central channel in four directions—front, back, left, and right—all perpendicular to the central channel. Then the branches keep bifurcating by twos. This branching, remember, is taking place in utero as the child is developing before birth. In this embryological development, 72,000 channels are formed throughout the entire body, and these 72,000 channels, including the central channel, right and left channels, and chakras, form the subtle body of each person.

When we die, this process all goes in reverse order. The channels, starting from the periphery (tips of toes and fingers), start reabsorbing more centrally. And eventually they make their way back to where they started, at the center of the chest, in the central channel at the heart chakra. Everything collapses sequentially inward at the time of death, leaving only the central channel with the heart chakra in the middle. As this happens, the energies enter the central channel, dissolve, and are absorbed into the central channel. Concurrently, the different sequential visions of the first four stages of the elements of the body dissolving appear. Finally, the visions of the last four stages, as the mind becomes progressively subtle, appear. This happens as the white essence in the central channel at the crown chakra descends, creating the white vision. Then the red essence from below ascends in the central channel, creating the red vision. When the two meet at the heart chakra, the black vision appears. When these two thoroughly mix at the heart chakra, the subtlest mind of clear light or luminosity appears. So as the elements dissolve, the energies enter, dissolve, and abide in the central channel, creating the first four visions.

FIG. 1

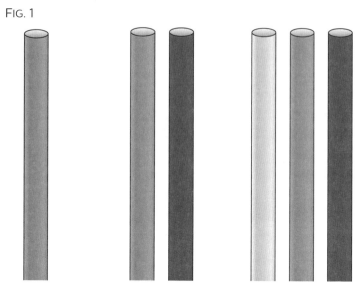

The left diagram shows the central channel, then with the right channel, then with both right and left side channels.

FIG. 2

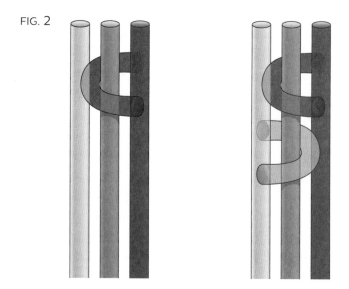

The left diagram shows the side channels wrapping around the central channel at the level of each chakra. The right shows the 3 wrappings from the sides channels at the heart chakra totaling 6.

FIG. 3

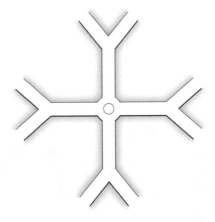

The diagrams shows the 4 branches from the central channel
(small circle in the middle); each of which branches again into 2;
again into 2; again into 2: and again into 2. The heart chakra has
the least branches (8), and the navel chakra the most (64).

Then, as the essences within the central channel descend from
top to bottom and ascend from bottom to top, the inner visions
of white, red, black, and clear light manifest to the dying person. Everybody has these experiences but may not recognize
them clearly, as there are so many things happening during
the death process that the ordinary person is distracted and
overwhelmed. The ordinary person is not trained to look for
these inner visions and work with them.

The yogi or yogini can also generate these experiences
through meditation and recapitulate the death experience.
Such profound meditation experiences come only through
long training. Just as an Olympic athlete does not reach the top
of his or her event in a couple of days, or even years, of training,
deep experiences of these inner visions through meditation

take long spiritual training and practice. The goal for the athlete is the gold medal. The goal for the meditator is unconditional love and the bliss of the completely perfect wisdom, knowing every existent thing fully and correctly. This knowledge is not only for the present, but for the past and future also. And not only for one's own mind, but knowledge of everyone's mind.

Knowing all there is to know is omniscience. This is the exceptional quality of enlightenment. It is not just knowledge for its own sake, but knowledge to guide countless living beings to this same state of enlightenment. When meditation on the channels and chakras, along with the resultant visions (as the energies enter, abide, and dissolve into the central channel), is done concurrently with what is happening naturally during the death process, some extraordinary things happen. When the natural death process involving eight stages reaches the eighth stage of clear light or luminosity, and the dying person is able to meditate on this stage and through the power of the meditation sustain the experience of clear light, this is called *thukdam*. This is the Tibetan term that literally means "sacred mind." *Thuk* is the honorific word for "mind" and *dam*, in this context, means "sacred." This refers to the subtlest mind of clear light or luminosity, called *woesel* (*od gsal*) in Tibetan and *prabhasvara* in Sanskrit. It is not until the eighth stage of clear light is finished that the subtle mind and subtle energy leave the gross body, which becomes a corpse. This is the actual time of death according to the Buddhist Vajrayana tradition. When a great practitioner enters the state of thukdam during the death process, the practitioner does not die but rather sustains this eighth stage, of clear light, remaining in a fresh, vibrant state, meditating on clear light. There are no signs of decomposition. What does this mean? I have seen this state three times, during the death process in three great meditators. In each case, these masters of meditation did not die for up to three weeks after their heart stopped beating, no blood pressure was recorded, and signs of breathing ceased. They were declared clinically dead. Nevertheless, they stayed alive. I have seen this. It is possible. It can be done when this meditation is done at the time of death. What I have not seen but which is even more amazing, is what is written in the great texts. When someone stays in this clear light meditation, extending their death, over time the body gradually shrinks. Eventually, all that is left is hair and nails and clothes—no hair in my case! I know this sounds strange, but this is what is written in the texts.

I was in Ulan Bator, Mongolia, at the Bogd Khan Jebtsundampa (reincarnations of the leader of Mongolian Buddhism, akin to the Dalai Lama of Tibet) museum. There was an embalmed body of a great teacher, who had been the tutor of the previous, previous Bogd Khan of Mongolia. His body, in the cross-legged sitting position, had shrunk to about twenty-four to thirty inches in height or maybe a little larger. Now this is Mongolia and in that time they did not embalm bodies using formaldehyde; they used salt. This draws out the liquid and there is some shrinking of the body from this process, but not that much. Not the kind of shrinking I witnessed with this Mongolian teacher. Of course he may have been a very, very short man while alive. Needless to say, I never saw him alive. The great texts go on to say that at the time of such a death there are arching rainbows filling the sky than can be witnessed by all for days or weeks. While in the state of thukdam the person does not die. A person who is able to sustain this mind of clear light state indefinitely will reach a deathless state, which we call enlightenment, or Buddhahood. This whole process, whereby a seasoned meditator actually meditates on the clear light as it is naturally manifesting during the end of the death process, is called "the meeting of the mother and child clear light."

The Buddhist understanding of death is a process comprised of eight stages. In the first four stages, each physical element dissolves into the next. As the body loses its power, the first four stages and the process of dissolving look like this:

1. earth, solid → dissolves or weakens
2. water, liquid → dissolves or weakens
3. fire, heat → dissolves or weakens
4. wind, kinetic energy → dissolves or weakens

"Dissolve" is not exactly what takes place, although the Tibetan word *thim* is usually translated as "dissolve." What is involved is the loss of power and the energy to maintain the solid elements of the body. As the solid elements of the body lose their power, the liquid elements (blood, spinal fluid, and such) gain more power relative to the earth elements.

When the dying person reaches the fourth stage, the wind, or kinetic energy, dissolves or loses its power. Thereby all movement dies down and eventually stops. There is no more blood circulation, hence no blood pressure. There is no more movement of air, hence respiration stops. If an EEG were to check for cortical brain activity, none would be found. At this fourth stage, modern medical doctors declare the person clinically dead. But from a Buddhist perspective, the individual still has a lot of life left in him or her. We still have to traverse the next four stages. At this point, it is the person's mind that dissolves into the next subtler one, or loses its power relative to the next subtler mind, in this order:

5. mind of whiteness → dissolves into
6. mind of redness → dissolves into
7. mind of blackness → dissolves into
8. the subtlest mind of clear light or luminosity

These are technical terms based in experience, although a very subtle experience. So let's see what Buddhist teachings say about what is going on at these last four stages of death. Recall the 72,000 channels in our bodies. Now, from the beginning of the death process at the first stage, these channels are gradually reabsorbing from the periphery of the body into the central channel. In the central channel are *essences*. In Sanskrit they are named *bindu*, while in Tibetan they are called *tigle*. Sometimes these essences are called *bodhicitta*, not to be confused with the universal compassion, although there is a connection, as subtler bodhicitta and sunyata experiences are brought about through the melting of these essences in the central channel. In English, some translators refer to these essences as a "drop." I am not a fan of the term "drop." A drop is nothing special. But these essences *are* something special, the bindu or tigle. They are the subtle essences of our life. It's like when a good cook uses the process of reduction to intensify the flavor of a sauce by simmering or boiling the sauce down to highlight its essence. They are the subtlest aspect of the body, or of the whole physical world for that matter. In the Kalachakra tantric system there is mention of *space particles*. These may be the subtlest aspect of matter, which may correlate with inner bindu or tigle. Even subtler than quarks! The bindu or tigle may be akin to what are mentioned in Kalachakra Tantra as *space particles*. These apparently are the most subtle aspects of matter. They may occur in universes just prior to the big bang, although this is hypothetical. Hence, within in the body, these bindu or tigle may be their inner world correlates.

When the white essence flows down from the crown chakra at the top of the central channel, it creates the inner vision of the mind of whiteness. This is the fifth stage of the death process. Similarly, when the red essence ascends up the central channel from the secret chakra at the genitals, it creates the inner vision of the mind of redness. This is the sixth stage. When these two (white and red essences) meet but have not yet fully dissolved into each other at the heart chakra within the central channel, this meeting creates the inner vision of a total blackout, followed by an experience of something almost like fainting but not actually leading to unconsciousness. This is the seventh stage. When these two essences fully merge, there comes a new vision of intense clarity unlike any previous human experience. We get tastes of it in normal life. Sometimes when we yawn or sneeze, we feel great joy. It also happens with sexual orgasm. But the joy or bliss we feel in sexual orgasm is miniscule in comparison to what is experienced through meditation; it is totally filled with attachment that blocks our experience of reality. The utter clarity of the mind of clear light, on the other hand, is unbound limitless joy and love experiencing reality directly. So there is no attachment at all. When these two white and red essences mix indistinguishably at the heart chakra as an "indestructible drop," this is the last, eighth stage of the death process. When this ends, as I mentioned above, that is the precise moment of death. The subtlest mind with its subtlest energy leaves the gross physical body, which now becomes a corpse and starts to decay.

I want to try to describe these eight stages of inner vision step by step, at least the way I imagine they might be.

The first stage when the solid elements are weakening, the inner vision is a mirage-like vision. Outwardly the dying person's body becomes heavy. It is difficult to move the arms and legs. There is a feeling of sinking into the bed. The sense of vision weakens. So when the solid element is weakening and the liquid element is becoming relatively stronger, then we get a vision like a mirage.

The second stage is when the liquid element is becoming weaker and the heat element is growing in strength; we get the inner vision of billowing smoke. Outwardly the dying person feels a strong thirst, which is not quenched by sips of water. The eyes recede back into the head. The skin loses its elasticity. If pinched, the skin stays "tented." The sense of hearing weakens.

During the third stage, when the heat element is weakening and the kinetic energy element is getting stronger, we get a vision of something like darting fireflies in the dark night, or perhaps a vision of sparks coming off the burning ember of a log in a dark night. The dying person experiences severe cold, which is not relieved by blankets. The sense of smell and taste weaken.

Then on the fourth stage, as the kinetic energy weakens and the consciousness element is becoming stronger, our inner vision becomes like a flame. It is not actually a flame but more like the last moments of a flickering flame before it goes out, more like the glow of an extinguishing candle in a jar. During the fourth stage the dying person has withdrawn all the senses grossly. As all movement within the body stops, so do the circulation of blood, movement of breath for respiration, and neuronal impulses in the brain and nervous system. At this stage the person is declared clinically dead. These are the first four stages.

The next four stages deal with the mind as it becomes more and more subtle, as these essences flow in the central channel. The fifth stage occurs with the white essence flowing down, and the dying person experiences a whiteness. This is called the mind of white appearance, something similar to the white of moonlight. The thing to keep in mind is that this is a point when the mind is becoming very subtle. We are moving beyond our normal understandings and concepts. The mind is becoming non-conceptual. We are moving beyond duality. So there is no sense of "me" and no sense of "moonlight" at this stage. It's as if we have *become* the moonlight. There is no recognition of any subject or object; there is just whiteness.

At the sixth stage, the red essence is flowing up and the dying person experiences a redness, something similar to the red of sunset. Again, this is a very subtle mind without any recognition of "me" or "sunset." Rather we *become* the redness. This is called the mind of red increase.

When the red and white essences meet at the heart chakra but have not fully merged, the dying person experiences an inner vision of blackness and a sensation similar to fainting, almost like losing consciousness. The person doesn't lose consciousness, but that is the sense of this stage. It is something similar to a total blackout without any rays of the moon or the sun. This is the seventh stage.

The darkness is followed by an utter clarity, which is the last, eighth stage, the mind of clear light. This is like an utter clarity not disturbed by moonlight, sunlight, or darkness. In Tibetan this is called od gsal, and in Sanskrit, prabhasvara. Another synonym in English is "luminosity." This is not a lightbulb. Again we are beyond duality and conceptuality and this stage is very subtle. It is more an intense mental clarity than a light. We are in a spiritual state far beyond conceptuality. So we don't have the language to do justice to these esoteric states. This is true particularly for the English language because the English-speaking world did not grow up with these kinds of concepts at the center of its culture. On the other hand, Pali, Sanskrit, and Tibetan all grew up within this spiritual context and have worked these ideas for millennia.

I use the diamond image because for me that represents utter mental clarity. And I think what this experience must be is an incredible degree of clarity in which there is no obstruction to our mind at all. It's as if the mind can see or experience *everything*. It's the mind, when sustained indefinitely, that goes on to become a Buddha who actually sees, or reaches understanding of, everything there is to be known.

From the Buddhist perspective, when the person dies, that is when this eight-stage process finishes. When the mind of clear light ends, that is when the mind with its subtlest energy separates from the body. And this is considered the actual moment of Buddhist death. The clear light mind then exits the body at the north—the crown of the head at the top of the central channel—or the south—through the body's lower orifices. And the texts tell us that if we have been a pretty good person, accumulating good deeds, then our rebirth will be a positive experience with less suffering and our subtle mind will exit from the top of the head, migrating to the upper of the six realms. However, if we have done harm and led a life of selfish concern, our subtlest mind-energy complex will exit from below and our rebirth will include greater degrees of suffering in the lower realms.

The mind then goes from gross to subtle in the reverse order, in what is called the *bardo,* or the intermediate state. This is an intermediate state between death and rebirth into another subtle energy body. This has similarities with the subtle dream body, which can leave the dreaming body and "fly" around without obstruction, only to return to the dreaming body before the person awakens from sleep. The bardo state can last up to forty-nine days but not longer in an ordinary person who has no control over this process. And in this time we take a mini-rebirth in what is called *bardo* in Tibetan, or "intermediate being" in English. The intermediate being has a subtle energy body that cannot be obstructed, so it can go through walls and even mountains. When it's born, so to speak, in this mini-rebirth, its process reverses the eight stages, moving from subtle to gross, just like a regular rebirth. This intermediate being is looking or scanning for an appropriate rebirth based on its previous actions, or karma. And when it finds it, it unites with the sperm and egg at conception, if it is one of the four types of rebirth that come from the union of a sperm and egg. This becomes the vehicle for rebirth. Before that, the bardo, or intermediate being, will die in seven days *if* a suitable karmic rebirth is not found. Then another bardo or intermediate being takes another mini-rebirth. This can happen a maximum of seven times, for a total of forty-nine days. Within that forty-nine-day period, a karmicly determined rebirth will definitely take place. Each time there is any type of death, the sequence moves from gross to subtle. And whenever there is any type of birth, the sequence reverses and moves from subtle to gross. This gives us an insight that ordinary birth is not so special. It is rather gross and course, lacking subtlety. The new life begins its life cycle following the eight stages, from subtle to gross, resulting in rebirth. Special persons who have attained high spiritual states in either this or former lives have control over their rebirth. For example, the current Dalai Lama has said that he will not take rebirth in Tibet if the military occupation is still in place. He would just be used as a puppet of the Chinese government and hence would not have the freedom to maximally benefit others. Advanced beings like the Dalai Lama can control where and when they are reborn. Bodhisattvas return to *samsara* in order to continue their service to humanity and the animal kingdoms, to help them fully eliminate their misery. The thirteenth Dalai Lama passed in 1933, but the current, fourteenth Dalai Lama was not born until 1935. Possibly the fourteenth Dalai Lama was reborn beyond this planet, to benefit others in other parts of the universe. This is only a supposition made in trying to explain the two-year discrepancy.

Samsara

Samsara (Sanskrit) means "cyclic existence" in English. Other English terms used to translate *samsara* include "transmigration," "karmic cycle," "wheel of existence," "reincarnation," and "cycle of aimless drifting." This is the concept that there is not just one life but a recurrence of birth, death, the intermediate state, and rebirth occurring over and over. This has profound implications. It means that the continuum of life has no beginning. It implies that the continuity of life can be understood as a continuum of oscillations of subtlety of mind and body. Let me explain using this diagram.

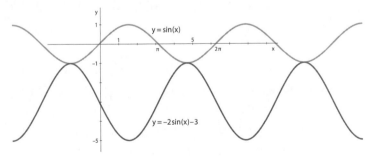

These two oscillating continuous curves
represent the continuity of life, or samsara.

The top sinusoidal (undulating) line represents our consciousness over time, while the bottom sinusoidal line represents our body over time. The diagram shows that from time to time there is a point of convergence. This is the moment of death, when the mind is in its most subtle aspect, as is the body. The space between convergence or touching points (i.e., death) represents life. This pattern of mental and energy oscillations from gross to subtle, subtle to gross, again and again, represents the continuity of life or samsara.

If we start to understand our lives that way, death is no big deal. I know this is not an easy thing for most of us to comprehend in this modern scientific culture, where to see is to believe, where death is taboo and kept out of polite discussions. But let me give some examples that might help:

- How big is the universe?
- How big are we?
- How long has the universe been around?
- How long are we going to be around?

From that perspective, we are inconsequential. And yet we make a big deal about dying. How silly is that? From the perspective of the continuity of mind represented by this energetic oscillation, we have been dying many times before. So another death is also no big deal.

Let me return to thukdam—the sustainability of the subtlest mind of clear light attained during the last portion of the dying process. Remember that this clear light mind state occurs naturally for all of us at the eighth stage of death. We usually miss it. But if we meditate at the time of our death, binding our meditation with the death process, we experience the *meeting of the mother and child (clear light mind)*; we sustain the clear light mind and its subtle body correlate. Thus we do not die. The body stays fresh and does not die. I have seen this three times. The body remains supple; there is no rigor mortis. There is a special subtle smell, like the faint smell of flowers or fruit, yet something new, never smelled before. That is my experience of being around three meditators in the state of thukdam. Being around the person in this state you feel joy. If you meditate around this person, your meditations are deeper and more powerful than usual. When thukdam continues even longer, beyond several weeks, the body of the great meditator reduces in size, as I mentioned above with the previous Bodg Khan, Jetsundampa.

What we learn from this is that meditators face their own death calmly with no regret, and even with joy. Many Tibetan Buddhist monks look forward to their death. Not as in a death wish but with the curiosity and unflinching conviction that meditating on the subtlest mind of clear light, as it naturally occurs just before death, can result in deep realizations on the path, even enlightenment. So they want to sustain this subtlest mind for as long as they can through uniting their death experience with meditation.

The revered Vietnamese Buddhist monk Thich Nat Hanh has this simple and profound saying: No death—No fear.

What might "no death" mean?

Everything changes moment to moment. This is just nature. Constant change is a natural part of life and the universe. Each new moment is fresh and alive, even the moment of so-called death. Now, that is a thought that goes against the grain of what most folks in the West believe. From the perspective of "no death, no fear," every moment, even the moment of death, is fresh and alive. It really means that there is no death. Death is a concept. So try to remember that when you are dying. Or when you are around people you love who are dying. Don't push any religion on them, but you can remind them of these positive things, that death is actually not so bad and that there is nothing to fear. Not only at the time of death but at every moment, remind yourself that each moment is new and fresh. There is nothing to fear. Change is a pillar of science as well. So try to move from theoretical understanding to experience. The implications are earth-shattering.

The best way to prepare for our death, for most people, is to practice love and compassion through generosity, patience, ethical discipline to avoid harm, perseverance, cultivation of a concentrated mind, and wisdom. The more love and compassion we put into our life, the easier our life will be and the easier our death will be.

Chapter 9

Meditation

Hard to restrain, unstable is the mind; it flits wherever it lists.
Good it is to control the mind.
A controlled mind brings happiness.
—The Buddha, cited in *Dhammapada*

As we have seen, one of the primary aims of Buddhist thought is to develop basic human qualities through transforming the mind. But to accomplish such a transformation, theoretical understanding is not enough. One also needs to practice. First we study and gain some intellectual knowledge. Then we marinate that understanding inside us. We begin to fuse it with our life, our way of thinking, our emotions, and our experience. Then we take it deeper through meditation, to stabilize our mind like a laser, then use this concentration to gain a nonconceptual, experiential understanding and realization that informs and merges with our inner life.

Our mind finds it very difficult to concentrate. It often wanders and jumps from place to place, seemingly out of our control. The term used for this phenomenon is "monkey mind," suggesting that the mind is like a monkey jumping here and there with no discipline. This wild mind is also likened to a wild elephant. The trainer, step by step, gradually subdues the wild elephant. This is analogous to the nine stages of mental quiescence cultivated through concentration meditation training.

In order for the mind to be able to concentrate, we need to calm the monkey down, allow our mind to become free of distractions such as the numerous thoughts, images, bodily sensations, feelings, and emotions that cause so much mental disturbance.

Monkey mind cannot sit still

Shamatha (concentration) meditation tames the wild distracted mind in 9 stages as seen here with the wild elephant and monkey gradually moving from black to white.

But how do we do that? We have to begin by making the mind stable and clear. My friend and fellow monk Matthieu Ricard gives the following example.[1] Suppose you are trying to retrieve a key that has fallen into a pond. If you poke about on the bottom of the pond with a stick, you will muddy the water and you won't be able to spot the key. The first thing you have to do is let the water settle until it becomes clear. After that it will be easy to see the key and pick it up. The same applies to the mind. We must first make it clear and calm. Then we will be able to develop the qualities of mind that lead to compassion and wisdom.

Two basic types of meditation are practiced in all Buddhist schools. There is *shamatha* (Sanskrit) or *shinay* (Tibetan), or "concentration," "focused," or "calm abiding" in English. Then there is *vipassana* (Sanskrit) meditation, in English "contemplative" or "analytical" meditation. Within each major category of meditation there are many subdivisions of techniques or practices. In this chapter I will discuss a number of meditation disciplines practiced in Buddhism.

The first type is concentration meditation. This means keeping our attention on the chosen object without distraction or dullness of mind. It essentially means focusing and brightening our mind. The objects we use to focus the mind are most commonly internal objects. The breath is the most common object we focus on to train our concentration. It could also be a mental image, such as a mental image of the Buddha. The mental image of the Buddha is visualized on the crown of our head or in front of us. It can even be imagined in our heart chakra—between the breasts, in the middle of our chest. If a Vajrayana form of the Buddha is chosen, then provided we've received empowerment, we can hold an image of our self in this form, called a *yidam* in Tibetan. The image can be the size of our palm or, when we get better, the size of our thumb or, when we get much better, the size of a sesame seed. If we've not received empowerment into a tantric deity practice, then we lack the prerequisites to visualize our self as the deity. Yet we can visualize the tantric deity at our crown, heart, or in front of us.

We can also choose to focus on our mind itself. This is more challenging. First we must identify the essential qualities of the mind. The two essential qualities of the mind are awareness and clarity. Awareness is experiencing—not experiencing anything in particular, rather just naked, bare experience. Clarity is the opposite of dullness. It refers to the mind, not to any object. When practicing mediation on the mind we drop our focus on any single object, yet we remain open to all. We abide in awareness, remaining alert with clarity. It becomes an open presence type of meditation. The mind, including the senses, remains wide open but without engaging anything. The mind remains alert, relaxed, and wide open, fixating on nothing. Slowly, with practice this mind will be infused with the wisdom of emptiness, not grasping at anything, as well as with unconditional compassion.

Or we may just remain in the present moment and not focus our mind on anything, yet stay alert and not fall asleep. With time bare awareness will flower. Of course it is always there but we cloud it with mental clutter. This process is like finding the deep, still ocean while letting go of the surface waves. Technically, the mind meditation is within the shamatha type of meditation, yet the mind does not focus on any object. So there is no reference point; none inside and none outside. It is common in the Zen practice of *Zazen*, and in the Tibetan Buddhist practices of *Mahamudra* and *Tsogchen*. So pick whichever object (or no object) is comfortable and stay with that object or objectless (at least unrecognized object) state.

If you have chosen a mental object, then stay with that image, size, and location for some time. If we constantly change our object or its size, color, or location, we will not cultivate mental stability and clarity. The image can also be one from another religion, for example, Jesus if you are a Christian or Brahma or Shiva if you are a Hindu.

Such focus is not easily accomplished. One will inevitably find that the mind will wander, much like a young puppy that one is trying to potty train. When the puppy leaves the paper, don't give up. Just gently return him to the paper; that is, when the mind wanders gently return to your focus on the breath or your image of the Buddha, et cetera. With continual practice over some time, usually months or years, the mind can be tamed just like taming a wild elephant or a hyperactive monkey.

As we begin daily practice concentrating our mind, the mind will begin to settle. For serious practice, we may do many short, fifteen-minute meditation sessions each day. Or due to many work and home responsibilities we may choose to do one session every morning. At the beginning our mind will mostly be distracted and off our chosen object. This is the first stage, in which the mind is mostly off the object. With practice the mind will reach the second level, in which the mind is equally on and off the chosen object. With more practice our mind will be mostly on the object, and with even more practice the mind will always be on the object, although part of the mind may still wander. These last two are the third and fourth stages. By this time we are really cooking. This is an amazing accomplishment that takes much effort, patience, and practice. Reaching the fourth stage is a landmark whereby stability is attained. This means the mind can now stay on its chosen object without getting distracted, for perhaps several hours. But stability is not yet complete.

We continue to make effort and meditate. After some time that portion of the mind that wandered while the rest of the mind stayed on the chosen object, settles down. In the fifth stage the mind is completely stable, so that the whole mind stays focused on the object. Then we start cultivating clarity of mind. When we reach the sixth stage, our mind is clear but not yet fully clear. There is still some dullness or sinking that is very difficult to recognize. With practice and persistence we can overcome this subtle laxity (dullness) in the seventh stage. At the eighth stage we have fully perfected stability and clarity of mind. But effort is still required. With further meditation we become so familiar that we no longer require effort. We just sit down with the intention to meditate on our object and automatically the mind is still—fully stable and clear. This is the ninth stage, called shamatha. This is a truly incredible accomplishment, but the process is still not complete.

We need to keep meditating and familiarizing our mind. Gradually, the energies in our body will smooth out and balance. In the context of shamatha meditation these energies are called "pliancies." The energies balance and centralize. Great joy is developed. It is not rough and excited, but rather subtle and steady, like placing a warm hand on a cleanly shaven head. Our body will feel light like a feather. Our seeing and hearing at distances will tremendously improve. Our mind becomes vaster, knowing others' minds not only in the present but also in the past and at times the future. Now we have prepared the mind to become serviceable. It becomes like a laser that penetrates and remains with utmost clarity on whatever wholesome topic we choose to meditate on, especially the Buddhist wisdom of emptiness.

The second type of meditation is contemplative, or analytical, meditation (*vipassana* in Sanskrit). There are many variations. We might analyze suffering, or compassion, or impermanence and death, or the wisdom of emptiness. These are all types of analytical meditation. Here we move from a peaceful state of mind to a state of deeper insight into the nature of the mind and the phenomenal world. This is accomplished by concentrating on a variety of mental phenomena, of which I will briefly mention three (there are many others). The goal of contemplative vipassana meditation is to become one with the quality meditated upon. For example, if we are meditating on compassion we try to feel or experience compassion. In this way we become compassion or compassionate.

One type of analytical meditation focuses on impermanence.

First there is *change*, or *impermanence*: I have a beautiful blue crystal vase. I am holding it; I drop it and it shatters. That crystal vase is demonstrating gross impermanence. It has come to the end of its continuum as a vase; it has broken. That is the meaning of gross impermanence. Gross impermanence is possible only because there is subtle impermanence. If phenomena did not change moment to moment, there would be no cause for their destruction. It is only because things arise and cease moment to moment that it is possible for a thing's continuum to cease; this is gross impermanence. Subtle impermanence is momentary change, something scientists know all about. Everything is changing from moment to moment. So we meditate on subtle impermanence. Very accomplished meditators can experience that momentary change, though it is not easy to do.

What is beneficial and healthy about meditating on impermanence is that at the time of your death the change you will be experiencing will be no big deal. You will realize that you are observing *only* momentary change, one moment to the next. We tend to see death as a fixed state, but that is our concept of death; it is not real. Practiced meditators are very good at identifying subtle change; all they see is one moment to the next. There is no death for them. This ability provides us with a much richer experience when we die and a much richer experience when we live. Every moment is fresh and new.

A second type of analytical meditation focuses on emptiness.

This is the quintessential topic for analytical meditation and indeed for the practice of finding the deepest happiness: *All roads lead to emptiness.* All other analytic meditations cultivate the foundation for our meditation on emptiness. These other practices of compassion and other desirable qualities gather merit. This merit will be the key to unlocking the understanding of emptiness. As we noted at the start of this book, the great soaring bird of enlightenment is held afloat by the two wings of wisdom and compassion. Emptiness is the most profound wisdom. Emptiness does not mean nothing exists. Rather it means that what we take to be real is mistaken. So things are empty of this distortion that they exist from their own side, that they have some essence or intrinsical reality, and that they exist independently or objectively. Thus our mental images (appearances) are not reality. There are no real and objective referents to our mental appearances. Everything lacks objectivity. This realization is pointed to by what we earlier referred to as "minding the gap." When we begin to understand that gap, we are coming close to understanding the meaning of emptiness. The gap between appearance and reality means that our appearances are not reality. They are only mental projections and distortions of reality.

The Buddha taught that there are two truths. This is how he would begin his discourses on emptiness. One is the deeper reality, or ultimate truth. This is emptiness. When we meditate on emptiness properly, nothing appears to the mind. But this is not mental "blankness" or "spacing out." Rather it is attentiveness to the absence of the appearing "I" or whatever object we choose for meditating on its emptiness. The other is conventional truth. As our understanding of ultimate reality deepens, so does our understanding of conventional truth. At first, conventional reality appears as our ordinary world. When we begin to understand the empty nature of things, then as we arise from meditation, appearances take on a dreamy, illusion-like quality. We see them but we know for sure they are not real. They lose their solid and objective feel. They lose their sense of being separate and independent from our mind. We slowly begin to realize they are merely imputed by our mind. There is nothing solid and objective out there.

So when we meditate on emptiness we first identify the object that mistakenly appears solid and objective. It appears independent. Then we negate that appearance in our meditation. Most analyses rely on the reasoning of "sameness or difference." We investigate whether the object we are investigating is the same as or different from its parts. For example, if we are meditating on our self, we investigate if our self is the same as the body and mind (called the aggregates), or completely different from the body and mind. If my self were identical to my body and mind, it would be senseless to assert a self, for it would be repetitious. Furthermore, if the self and body and mind are identical, then as there are two—body and mind— there must be two selves. Or as there is only one self, there can be only one, either body or mind. Moreover when the body dies the self would also have to die; but the self reincarnates, according to Eastern traditions. Also actions performed would be lost, since without a self there would be no place for the residua of actions to ripen. And the effects of actions not done would be encountered, since the self and hence the karma would be discontinuous. Effects of actions would be ripening on another continuum that did not produce the cause. If the self were separate from the aggregates, it could not possess the characteristics of the aggregates. Then we could not say "my body" or "my mind." We could not say, "my body is sick" or "my heart aches." These statements would be ridiculous if the self were in no way connected to the body and mind.

As we familiarize with this way of thinking, we gradually recognize that neither option described above is possible. As there is no third alternative, it begins to dawn on us that the only conclusion is that this self or ego we are analyzing does not exist. When this strikes home, we may spontaneously grab our clothing in fear, thinking we don't exist at all! With time, however, this fear morphs into joy and freedom. We begin to recognize that it is only the mistaken appearance of "my self" that does not exist. There still is a convention "my self." I haven't completely disappeared.

So gradually, with repeated meditation on emptiness, all these mistaken appearances dissolve. We are left with nothing appearing to the mind. This experience of emptiness is like space. When we arise from our meditation, everything we perceive has this illusory-like quality. Everything appears like an image in a dream upon awakening. Everything appears like a reflection in a mirror. Everything appears like water in a mirage, or like the sound of an echo. We see things but are convinced they are not real. This frees us from our ego's clinging because there is no more solid, independent ego to cling. But our conventional "self" still does exist.

Ego and compassion are inversely related like a teeter-totter or balance scale; as ego decreases, love and compassion automatically increase. This love and compassion arising from realizing emptiness has no strings attached. It is totally unconditional and unbiased. Nothing is expected in return. Since there is no one to expect anything, and nothing to expect, there is no expectation. This type of love and compassion is all-encompassing and profound. There is no more separation between them and us. Of course there are still others and there is still me, but not at all in the way we previously understood and experienced. We are all intimately connected. A radical transformation in our view takes place. A radical transformation in our life takes place. All our ordinary appearances dissolve in this selfless, empty state. A saying from the Buddha's *Aryaratnakarasutra* teachings puts it well: "Whatever is empty and cannot be perceived is like the tracks of a bird in the expanse of the sky."

There is utter joy infused with complete concern for others' welfare, love, and compassion. These are the experiences of the great masters of yesterday and today.

A third type of analytical meditation is investigating suffering.

When we cultivate a deeper understanding of our own suffering through analytical meditation, we are naturally led closer to the suffering of others. This naturally leads to the wish to relieve others' suffering. And this feeling is compassion, both for our self and for others. The Buddha taught three types of suffering, from the obvious to the less obvious to the hidden subliminal. The obvious suffering known to people as well as animals is physical and mental pain, dissatisfaction, and discontent. An example is physical pain, or emotional hurt and sadness. We all know this form of suffering. Slightly less obvious is the suffering of change. This is when pleasure ends and we don't like it. Or worse, when pleasure turns into pain. An example of the first is a lovely weekend spent with friends. When Monday rolls along, we have to go back to work or school. An example of the second is an "all you can eat" buffet dinner. The food tastes great, so we eat and eat and eat. By evening time we develop a stomachache due to indigestion and overeating.

Hidden subliminal suffering, the third type, is called "all-pervasive conditioned" suffering. This is difficult for all of us to recognize. Nevertheless, it fuels all the other suffering, so it is essential to identify it and learn ways to eradicate it. With eradication of the deepest form of suffering comes total freedom and joy. It is the wisdom of realizing emptiness that is the means to do this. This "all-pervasive" conditioned suffering is always with us, hence "all-pervasive." It is "conditioned" by our ignorance and is our default state of mind—dissatisfied and discontent. In German we call this "angst." It is like anxiety and fear, from which many of us are not free much of the time. This ignorance is the distorted ignorance of not knowing correctly who we are and what the world is. Ignorance is the exact opposite of emptiness. Emptiness is reality, the true nature of who we are and what the world is.

So by reflecting on these three types of suffering again and again, we naturally move toward understanding others' predicaments. This moistens our heart and moves us in the direction of compassion. The vehicle for this unconditional love and compassion is the understanding of emptiness—knowing reality as it is.

A fourth type of analytical meditation is compassion meditation.

Compassion means an orientation toward alleviating suffering. This is similar to love, which is an orientation toward bringing happiness. Both attitudes want happiness for others as well as for oneself. The more we reduce our self-preoccupation, the more our concern for others automatically grows, just like the teeter-totter or balance scale I mentioned earlier. One method of meditating on compassion is to recognize kindness shown to us by others. Normally we think only those we are close to and love show us kindness. This method of developing closeness toward others by recognizing their kindness toward us has been discussed above. To recap, we conceptually divide all others into three groups—those we feel close to, strangers, and enemies. Recognizing kindness in those we feel close to is easy, as we already do. Then extend the exercise to strangers. Here we consider all the things in our life that keep us alive, healthy, and thriving that came from the efforts of strangers. Then enemies have the potential to help us grow by actually becoming our teachers. They teach us patience instead of anger. Repeatedly thinking this way, gradually we feel closer to everyone. From feeling close to others to wanting them to be free of pain and be happy, is now a much smaller step.

The practice of *metta* [Pali], or loving-kindness meditation, begins with the meditator cultivating benevolence, or compassion, toward oneself; then toward one's loved ones, friends, teachers, strangers, and enemies; and finally toward all living beings. This is a variation of the recognizing-kindness-in-others meditation. Both have the outcome of making us feel closer to others. Modern instruction for the cultivation of compassion is based in part on a method found in Buddhaghosa's fifth-century text, the *Path to Purification* (Pali: *Visuddhimagga*).

There is also the practice of contemplating the *Brahmaviharas*, also called the four immeasurables, which is a form of compassion meditation. The four immeasurables are described below:

◆ Loving-kindness (Pali: *metta*; Sanskrit: *maitri*) toward all—the wish that others be well.

◆ Compassion (Pali and Sanskrit: *karuna*)—the wish that others' suffering will diminish.

◆ Empathetic joy (Pali and Sanskrit: *mudita*)—joy in the accomplishments of oneself and others. This is also referred to as sympathetic joy.

◆ Equanimity (Pali: *upekkha*; Sanskrit: *upeksa*)—learning to accept gain and loss, reputation and disgrace, praise and blame, pleasure and pain equally and with nonattachment, for oneself and for others. Detaching from these four pairs is also found in the practice of equalizing the eight world concerns. That is, having no attachment to reputation or defamation, to praise or blame, to gain or loss, to pleasure or pain.

Meditating on these four immeasurables again and again moistens the mind and moistens the heart, bringing more love and compassion.

Equalizing our reactions to both feelings in each of the four pairs can come about by practice, making effort. But these cannot be fully equalized without the practice of wisdom. The practice of wisdom allows us the full freedom of nonattachment. Being no longer attached to our ego, in fact recognizing there is no ego as we relate to it, these emotions of reputation and unknown, et cetera, completely lose their power. The wind is completely taken out of their sails, as there are no more sails and no more wind.

The full, complete form of compassion is unconditional, unbiased universal compassion, called *Bodhicitta* in Sanskrit. As there is no precise and complete term in English, we often keep it in Sanskrit. Bodhicitta has two parts: (1) the wish to become fully enlightened, and (2) for the purpose of bringing all beings to the same enlightened state. *Tonglen* in Tibetan means literally, "taking and giving." This means taking away suffering from everyone and giving back wisdom and compassion to all. This includes oneself. It is a practice to cultivate reducing our selfishness and increasing our love and compassion for others. It radically shifts the focus in our life. The meditation is done by breathing naturally through the nose with the mouth closed. When we breathe in, we imagine taking all the suffering from everyone including ourselves in the form of "dark smoke" as it comes in our nostrils and moves down to our heart chakra (middle of the chest). When it reaches our heart chakra it is immediately transformed into light, in the nature of love and wisdom energy—wisdom that is the source of unconditional love and compassion. Then we breathe out, sending this light-love-wisdom energy to fill all living beings including our self. It is very important that all the suffering be transformed at our heart into love and wisdom, without leaving behind in us any residual suffering. When we realize the empty nature of suffering it cannot hurt us. But before we realize emptiness, massive residual suffering from countless beings left in us can be overwhelming. So fully transform this inhaled suffering into positive energy. When we breathe out, that light-love-wisdom energy fills everyone, including ourselves. If you find that some of the suffering is sticking, then modify the Tonglen practice. Instead of breathing in the entire suffering, imagine it is being released through the crown of all beings, high into the stratosphere. You imagine this as you are breathing in. Then breathe out as before.

We can do this meditation targeting one or several individuals who are hurting. This can be done for one or several breaths. Then we expand our focus until we include everyone. One way to do this is by gradually expanding to larger and larger communities. We can start with those in our neighborhood, maybe in our room or building, then extend out to the community, the town, the city, and maybe to the region, then the country, the whole earth. We extend out above the earth to the birds and below the earth to the fish. Keep extending with each breath out to the solar system, galaxies, and then the universe and multiverse, everywhere there might be living beings.

Focused shamatha meditation on the breath

So let us start with a brief walk through a shamatha meditation. Sit up with your back straight and while you sit up straight relax your shoulders. Keep them straight but let them drop. This allows us to balance being alert with being relaxed. Try to meditate with our eyes open. If you can't do it with your eyes open, you can close them, but try with your eyes open. Later on, eyes open during meditation will bring more clarity to your meditation. This is how His Holiness the Dalai Lama meditates and teaches. This is also what we see on the old statues of the Buddha in meditation: eyes open and glancing down.

Keep your head straight, but with your eyes glancing down about one meter (yard) in front of you or a similar comfortable distance.

Try to have a soft gaze—whatever you see, try not to engage it. Try not to bore a hole with your eyes. Do not focus on anything with your eyes. This is what is meant by "soft gaze." This may take some time and practice. If you have trouble, try bringing your focal point somewhere between your eyes and whatever you are seeing. Often, this takes practice but it is

Barry meditating with three classes of third
graders in an American elementary school.

worth cultivating. If it simply doesn't work, you can close your
eyes, but try not to doze off.

And then I want you to focus just below your nose, at the
opening of the nostrils. This is done with your mind, not your
eyes. You don't want to end up cross-eyed. Just place your attention there, like an anchor.

You need to keep your mouth closed and breathe normally.
The air passes in and out through the nose. I want you to focus
on that sensation of the air passing at the base of the nose. I
don't want you to follow your breath all the way in and all the
way out. Not that. Rather just anchor your mind by keeping it
focused at the base of your nose. Remember not to force your
breath, but keep it relaxed and natural.

Balance between alertness and relaxation. Not too alert and
not too relaxed, but balanced. This balanced approach is not
just for meditation, but also for life in general. We balance by
avoiding the two extremes. In life in general, the two extremes
are extravagance and asceticism. In meditation, the two extremes

are being too alert or uptight and too relaxed or sleepy. In the understanding and realization of wisdom, the two extremes are reification and nihilism. There will be more about that below.

Now, you may get distracted. There may be a sound, a gurgling in your stomach saying, "When is dinner?" You may get a thought, a feeling, a bodily sensation, and your mind may go away from focusing on the breath at the base of the nose. Recognize that you are distracted and just bring your mind back to the base of the nose. You may have to do that many times—no problem. That is the work of meditation. That is the mental training. That is precisely meditation. It familiarizes us by training the mind to stay on the chosen object.

Place the hands with the palms facing up. The left hand is below and the right hand is on top, the thumbs pointing up to make a triangle, and then just rest your hands, in this position, in your lap. This is the common hand position you'll see in statues and paintings of the Buddha while meditating. Statues of the Buddha in meditation depict him with his eyes partially open, and gazing down as I mentioned before. Relax your shoulders. In meditation, and in fact in whatever we do, we try to balance being alert with being relaxed. If we are too alert, our mind will be excited and become easily distracted. If we are too relaxed, our mind will become dull or even fall asleep.

So find a quiet place and spend five or ten minutes, or longer if you are comfortable, every morning practicing this meditation; make it a habit. You do not need to set an alarm; this is only a distraction: "When are my five minutes up?" If you are comfortable going longer that is fine. Please do not push and end your session exhausted. Then you are too much on the alert side, and the next day you may find other things than meditation to do. Also please do not judge your meditation: "This was a good one," or "This was terrible, I am hopeless." Many things happen during meditation, such as purification, so it is hard to judge success anyway. It is a very good thing to do for yourself; a wonderful way to take good care of yourself. With some practice, your experience will ripple out to others and bring them some calmness and peace of mind. It may even bring to some of those around you inspiration to meditate, themselves.

In 2004, highly respected research articles began to appear in the best scientific journals, describing changes in the function and structure of the brains of long-term meditators. These findings were, and are, being published in the top neuroscience journals such as the *Proceedings of the National Academy of Science (PNAS)*, *Nature*, and others.[2] Meditators were at times placed in function magnetic resonance imaging (fMRI) machines. At other times they were hooked up to research electroencephalography (EEG). They were asked to meditate in the style of focused awareness (FA), or at other times in the style of open monitoring (OM). Open monitoring is similar to the *shamatha* meditation on the mind, that is, meditation on awareness itself, in which the mind and senses are wide open but not fixating on anything. Third, meditators were asked to meditate on open presence infused by compassion.

The changes in the brain occurred primarily during the open presence, with and without compassion. Such changes include alterations in patterns of brain function assessed with functional magnetic resonance imaging (fMRI), changes in the cortical evoked response to visual stimuli that reflect the impact of meditation on attention, and alterations in amplitude and synchrony of high-frequency oscillations (gamma waves), which probably play an important role in connectivity among widespread circuitry in the cortex of the brain.

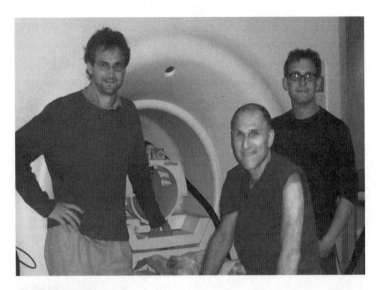

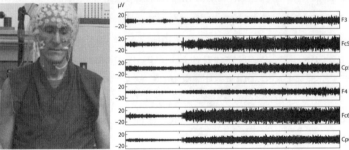

(top) Barry is smiling after spending about 2 hours in the fMRI machine. Regardless of the noise he was meditating.

(above left) Barry is meditating while hooked up to the EEG.

(above right) The EEG tracing demonstrates burst of gamma waves during meditation, particularly open presence and open presence with compassion. These high amplitude high frequency gamma waves occurred throughout the cortex during meditation suggesting synchronicity.

The state of open monitoring meditation may be best understood in terms of a succession of dynamic global states. Such synchronizations may play a crucial role in the development of transient networks that integrate distributed neural processes into highly ordered cognitive and affective functions. In other words, *global brain gamma wave activity may represent transient neural networks throughout the brain that enhance our awareness and well-being.* The functional MRI data showed amazing changes in the prefrontal cortex (PFC) of the brain, basically the whole forehead portion of the cortex. The cortex is the outer 1.5 centimeters of the brain and accounts for higher levels of functioning. The prefrontal cortex is called the executive function, or control center, for it is here primarily that planning, creativity, imagination, compassion, a sense of who we are (although not identity), and prosocial behavior occur. In long-term meditators the PFC is anatomically bigger and functionally more active than in nonmeditators. The EEG studies showed bursts of gamma wave activity throughout the cortex, strongly suggesting synchronicity across the cortex—front, back, right, and left. This is novel and not found in the neurology textbooks. Interestingly, synchronicity is the experience of the long-term meditator while meditating and sometimes when not meditating.

Chapter 10

Conclusion: Bringing It All Together

Let one's thoughts of boundless love pervade the whole world—
above, below, and across—without any obstruction,
without any hatred, without any enmity.

—The Buddha, from the *Metta-Sutta*

The Practice of Compassion

The practice of compassion is very special, for it is the road to happiness. When we practice love and compassion we feel good, "like a million bucks." But money cannot buy that deep inner feeling of well-being, joy, and tranquility. People and animals toward which we practice compassion also reap the benefits of our concern and help. Practicing compassion is multifaceted. Firstly, there is compassion to our self, taking good care of our self. Many of us neglect caring for our self. Love and compassion start at home. So taking good care of our self then ripples out to others. Eventually when we train in the

119

practice of unconditional love and compassion, our love and compassion go out equally to all living beings. This becomes an attitude, a way of life filled with meaning and joy.

Often it is difficult to practice compassion directly. There is some hesitancy, some resistance. Practicing generosity breaks down some of that resistance. It opens our heart, making us want to give more. Being mindful by observing our human experience, thoughts, emotions, and sensations allows us a golden opportunity. When harmful emotions arise, if we recognize them, with practice we can work on them. Eventually we will be able to transform them into their positive opposites. We all get angry, yet we do not like being angry. Recognizing anger early, we can embrace it and later replace it with its opposite antidote, tolerance or patience. This practice of reducing anger also opens our heart, allowing us to practice more love and compassion. These are the practices of moral discipline, of not harming, and of patience. They too open our heart and allow us to practice more love and compassion.

If you are always in the distracted multitasking mode, you'll not accomplish much. So the practice of "not giving up" becomes important for accomplishing worthwhile goals. This is the practice of perseverance. A scattered mind is not very efficient. It does not move us forward. Rather it moves us in all directions, right, left, front, back, up, and down. So we get nowhere. A more concentrated, focused mind, on the other hand, gives us clarity, perspective, and thus momentum to move forward with worthwhile activities. "Not giving up" when we are doing worthwhile activities also opens our heart, allowing us to practice more love and compassion.

Last, seeing reality, including our ego, as it is, not inflated or deflated, adds tremendous depth and joy to whatever we do. It is as if the clouds of our mind open up to the mind of vast blue sky. This practice of wisdom also opens our heart and allows us to practice more love and compassion. When we are able to combine some sense of an illusory-like, dream-like reality of our experience with the above practices of giving, morality, tolerance, perseverance, and concentration, then these practices become very powerful. Take, for example, giving. Try to see the giver (our self), the one to whom we are giving (recipient), and the action of giving all like illusions; this makes giving and all the other practices much more powerful. In Buddhist parlance these become perfect practices—the six *paramitas* [Sanskrit], or "perfections" in English—because they are no longer deluded by ignorance. They also help us find our inner moral compass.

Finding Our Inner Moral Compass

Integrity and honesty become our moral compass, pointing us always in the right direction of love, compassion, and wisdom. Honesty nourishes self-confidence, a healthy self-confidence that neither puts me down nor puts you down. This brings the courage to practice compassion and respect for others, regardless of their opinions or actions. Of course if others are harming through bullying, abuse, or bigotry, our response is to do what we can to help the situation. In this way compassion is active and engaged, not passive and weak. But it does not involve anger or hatred. Nelson Mandela practiced this way. So did Martin Luther King and Mahatma Gandhi. And of course the His Holiness the Dalai Lama is the inner moral compass for the entire world, including the Chinese. There are more than 400 million Chinese who say they are Buddhist.

Beyond Empathy

Empathy is feeling what the other person is feeling. When every day we are around people or animals that are hurting, it can be overwhelming. Empathy, or feeling others' pain, can stick in our heart, making us feel sad, overwhelmed, depressed, and burnt out. So it is important to move beyond empathy to compassion. Compassion is the wish and action to help others relieve their suffering. While it is tinged (His Holiness the Dalai Lama uses this word) with sadness, the overarching feeling of compassion is joy; the joy of helping, even trying to help regardless of outcome. So there is no guilt. We do the best we can, and that is enough. Most of us, after doing ten things in a day, remember only the two or three that did not go as we wished. We forget the other seven or eight that went well. So a reality check to remember all ten is healthy. In this way, we are taking good care of our self and also reducing guilt.

Never Give Up

In a few compassion "hot spots" around the world, such as Dharamsala, one can see T-shirts with the following message on the back: "Never Give Up." These powerful words from His Holiness the Dalai Lama bring us inspiration to believe, "I can do it!" It brings us courage to try to be a better human being.

We all are mixtures of positive and negative. Remember the story of Atisha that I told before about the piles of black and white stones.

By trying to practice becoming more positive and happy, we can succeed; not with one big step, rather with many small steps. Of course it takes time. Usually our negative habits are deep-seated within us, often since childhood. So overturning them—not suppressing them—also will take time. You can do it, with patience, courage, and an attitude of not giving up: "I CAN DO IT!"

If you think you are too small to make a difference, try spending a night with a mosquito!

Notes

CHAPTER I

1. Books by Gem Lamrimpa:

— *Calming the Mind: Tibetan Buddhist Teachings on the Cultivation of Meditative Quiescence* (Ithaca, NY: Snow Lion, 1992).

— *Samatha Meditation: Tibetan Buddhist Teachings on the Cultivation of Meditative Quiescence* (Ithaca, NY: Snow Lion, 1993).

— *Transcending Time: An Explanation of the Kalachakra Six-Session Guruyoga* (Somerville, MA: Wisdom Publications, 1999).

— *Realizing Emptiness: Madhyamaka Insight Meditation* (Ithaca, NY: Snow Lion, 2002).

— *How to Realize Emptiness* Quiescence (Ithaca, NY: Snow Lion, 2010).

CHAPTER 3

1. Dalai Lama, His Holiness, *How to See Yourself as You Really Are* (New York: Atria Books, 2006).

2. Dalai Lama, His Holiness,, *Kindness, Clarity, and Insight* (Ithaca, NY: Snow Lion, 2006).

CHAPTER 4

1. B. L. Andersen et al., "Psychological Intervention Improves Survival for Breast Cancer Patients," *Cancer* 113 (2008): 3450–3458.

2. T. W. Pace et al., "Effect of Compassion Meditation on Neuroendocrine, Innate Immune and Behavioral Responses to Psychological Stress," *Psychoneuroendocrinology* 34, no. 1 (Jan 2009): 87–98.

3. L. Carlson, "Mindfulness-based Cancer Recovery and Supportive-Ex-

pressive Therapy Maintain Telomere Length Relative to Controls in Distressed Breast Cancer Survivors," *Cancer* 121, no. 3 (2014): 476–484.

4. Barry Kerzin, TEDx Talk Phoenixville: "Seeing Kindness in All Others," July 10, 2010, https://www.youtube.com/watch?v=FY1g-e1BlYc#].

5. Norman Cousins, *Anatomy of an Illness as Perceived by the Patient: Reflections on Healing* (New York: W. W. Norton, 2005).

CHAPTER 5

1. Shantideva, *A Guide to the Bodhisattva's Way of Life*, trans. B. Alan Wallace (Ithaca, NY: Snow Lion, 1997).

CHAPTER 6

1. Dalai Lama, *Beyond Religion: Ethics for a Whole World* (New York: Houghton Mifflin Harcourt, 2011).

2. This comment by Dr. Paul Ekman came during a private discussion with His Holiness the Dalai Lama outside Chicago, around 2012, to which I was invited. See Paul Ekman and Richard J. Davidson, *The Nature of Emotion: Fundamental Questions* (Oxford: Oxford University Press, 1994).

3. Shantideva, *A Guide to the Bodhisattva's Way of Life* (Dharamsala, India: Library for Tibetan Works and Archives, 1999), chap. 5, v. 13.

4. Singer, T., Bolz, M., *Compassion: Bridging Compassion and Science* (Munich: Max Planck Society eBook, 2013), chapters 4 and 9.

CHAPTER 7

1. Dalai Lama, His Holiness, *How to See Your Self as You Really Are* (New York: Atria Books, 2006).

2. Barry Kerzin, *Nagarjuna's Wisdom: A Guide to Practice*, forthcoming.

3. See also the translation of *Nagarjuna's Fundamental Wisdom of the Middle Way*, trans. by Jay L. Garfield (Oxford: Oxford University Press, 1995).

4. Mark Siderits and Shoryu Katsura, *Nagaruna's Middle Way* (Somerville, MA: Wisdom Publications, 2013).

5. See by Rje Tsong Khapa, *Ocean of Reasoning: A Great Commentary on Nagarjuna's Mulamadhyamakakarika*, trans. by Jay L. Garfield and Geshe Ngawang Samten (Oxford: Oxford University Press, 2006).
6. David Darling, *Zen Physics: The Science of Death, The Logic of Reincarnation* (First Edition Publishing, 2012), see chap. 10.
7. Ibid., p. 131.

CHAPTER 9
1. *Why Meditate*, p. 54.
2. A. Lutz et al., "Long-term Meditators Self-induce High-amplitude Synchrony During Mental Practice," *Proceedings of the National Academy of Sciences* 101 (2004):16369–16373.

Further Reading

CHAPTER 3

Hopkins, Jeffrey. *Mediation on Emptiness*. Somerville, MA: Wisdom Publications, 1983/1996.

Thurman, Robert. *The Central Philosophy of Tibet: A Study and Translation of Je Tsongkhapa's "Essence of True Eloquence."* Princeton: Princeton University Press, 1984.

Thurman, Robert, and William Meyers. *Man of Peace: The Illustrated Life Story of the Dalai Lama of Tibet*. New York: Tibet House US, 2017.

Tsongkhapa and Josua Cutler. *The Great Treatise on the Stages of the Path to Enlightenment*. Ithaca: Snow Lion, 2002.

Yeshe, Thubten. *Wisdom Energy: Basic Buddhist Teachings*. Somerville, MA: Wisdom Publications, 1982/2012.

CHAPTER 8

Dalai Lama (trans. Jeffrey Hopkins), *Advice on Dying: And Living a Better Life* (New York: Atria Books, 2002).

Lati Rinpoche and Jeffrey Hopkins, *Death, Intermediate State and Rebirth in Tibetan Buddhism* (Ithica, NY: Snow Lion, 1981).

Sogyal Rinpoche, *The Tibetan Book on Living and Dying* (New York: HarperCollins, 2002).

CHAPTER 10

Dalai Lama, *Freedom in Exile: The Autobiography of the Dalai Lama* (New York: Harper Perennial, 1991 and 2008).

Dalai Lama, *The Universe in a Single Atom: The Convergence of Science and Spirituality* (New York: Morgan Road Books, 2006)

About the Author

THE VENERABLE DR. BARRY KERZIN is an Affiliate Professor at the University of Washington, Tacoma, a Visiting Professor at Central University of Tibetan Studies in Varanasi, India, an Honorary Professor at the University of Hong Kong (HKU), and a former Assistant Professor of Medicine at the University of Washington. Dr. Kerzin is also a fellow at the Mind and Life Institute and consults for the Max Planck Institute in Leipzig on compassion training.

He is the founder and president of the Altruism in Medicine Institute (AIMI) **www.altruismmedicine.org** and the founder and chairman of the Human Values Institute (HVI) in Japan **www.humanvaluesinstitute.org.**

Since 1989, he has been providing free medical care to the poor up to the highest lamas, including the Dalai Lama. Dr. Kerzin has completed many meditation retreats, including a three-year retreat. His brain was studied at Princeton University and the University of Wisconsin, Madison as a long-term meditator. He was ordained as a monk by the Dalai Lama and combines his work as a monk and doctor, harmonizing the mind and body. He lectures around the world in Japan, Europe, North America. Hong Kong, Taiwan, Korea, Russia, and Mongolia.

He has written *Tibetan Buddhist Prescription for Happiness,* and with the Dalai Lama and Prof. Tonagawa, *Mind and Matter: Dialogue between Two Nobel Laureates,* in Japanese. His book, *Nagarjuna's Wisdom: A Guide to Practice* is in-press. He has written chapters for many books including *Compassion: Bridging Practice and Science* from the Max Planck Institute. He has written many articles and has given many interviews for radio, and TV, including documentaries on PBS New Medicine 2005, PBS Ethics and Religion 2015 and PBS NewsHour.

For more information on Dr. Kerzin's work, visit:
www.altruismmedicine.org

and follow on Twitter at:
#aimicompassion

100% of the royalties will go to the nonprofit organization Altruism in Medicine Institute